ONE MAN'S WAR

ONE MAN'S WAR

BY

Frank Stroobant

B PUBLICATIONS DIVISION

BURBRIDGE LIMITED

ONE MAN'S WAR

First Edition — 15,000 — March, 1967
Second Edition — 10,000 — July, 1970
Third Edition — 20,000 — May, 1974
Fourth Edition — 7,500 — June, 1980
Corgi Edition — 20,000 — 1981

Burbridge First Edition — 7,500 — 1984
Second Edition — 15,000 — 1985
Third Edition — 5,000 —1988
Fourth Edition — 5,000 — 1990
Fifth Edition — 5,000 — 1992
Sixth Edition — 2,000 — 1997

ISBN 0 950360 1 4

Published by Burbridge Ltd.,
Les Câches, St. Martin's, Guernsey, C.I.

Printed by the Guernsey Press Co. Ltd., Guernsey, C.I.

ACKNOWLEDGMENTS

Sir Ambrose Sherwill, K.B.E., M.C., for the Foreword.

Ronald Seth, Esq., for his advice during writing the book.

Colin Cowdrey, Esq., for his encouragement and efforts to find a publisher.

The Directors and Staff of the Publishers for their interest and co-operation, in particular Messrs. H. N. Machon, F. S. Roussel, V. D. Symes, C. S. Gardner, C. Toms, G. K. Anderson.

Joseph Mackiewicz, author of "Katyn Wood Murders."

Printed by The Guernsey Press Co., Ltd.
8, Smith Street, St. Peter Port,
Guernsey, Channel Islands.

CONTENTS

ILLUSTRATIONS

This book is dedicated to my late wife, Gladys, who, like many thousands of other women, was left to provide for herself and family during this tragic period. Her courage, determination and faithfulness will always be remembered by me with love and admiration.

Schloss Laufen, Bavaria

FOREWORD

by

SIR AMBROSE SHERWILL, K.B.E., M.C.

"ONE MAN'S WAR" is a scrupulously honest account of the heartaches, frustrations, experiences and achievements of a Guernseyman, who, remaining in Guernsey at the time of its occupation by the Germans in 1940, did his utmost to be of service to his fellow islanders and, being eventually deported to Germany and interned there, continued faithfully to serve his fellow internees.

I can make no estimate of the generality of its appeal but it will, I am confident, be of absorbing interest to all who in any way shared his experiences. Many of the happenings of which he writes have not hitherto been recorded and his account of life in the internment camps at Dorsten and Laufen is both accurate and informative.

I was not deported until February, 1943, and so escaped the hardships of Dorsten. When I arrived at Laufen, the camp, with Frank Stroobant as British Camp Senior, was extremely well organised and I settled in as an ordinary internee for, as I anticipated, the duration. His eminently reasonable proposals for the conservation of Red Cross supplies produced such animosity that, in June of that year, he resigned and—to my surprise—I was elected to succeed him.

Now, it is a fundamental principle of English law that "The King can do no wrong". I quickly came to appreciate that in an internment camp—at least in ours—the Camp Senior can do nothing right. As a result of some bitter experiences, I learned to treat it as a normal reaction and henceforth lost no sleep. Perhaps, in the enforced idleness and the consequential boredom and frustrations, it was essential—or at least desirable—that there should be a scapegoat who could be blamed for the overcrowding, discomforts, incompatibilities of temperament and other annoyances to which internees were subjected.

By the time I took over, there had been a complete change of German staff. The Commandant, the Security Captain, the Senior Sonderführer and the Camp Doctor were all pleasant people and appeared to be genuinely concerned with the welfare of the internees. I had to visit the German Camp Office daily and the bulk of my business was transacted with the senior Sonderführer who had been at school in England and was a most capable administrator with iron nerves. It was, I knew, the general view among internees that he was much too "fly" for a simple soul like me. I can only say that he never once let me down.

Our news service, based entirely on Frank Stroobant's nightly vigils with the home-made receiver did much to maintain our morale and we largely disregarded the German news in English available on the loud-speaker in our canteen.

Early in March, 1945, Feldwebel Ertl made an intensive search of the camp and unearthed masses of things we were not supposed to have. He failed, however, to find what he was looking for, *i.e.* our wireless set! Then the Sonderführer sent for me and told me that, from the things internees wrote in their letters home and which were, of course, censored out, they knew we must have a wireless receiver but could not find it. Something—he would not tell me what—was about to happen. If our set was discovered, one result might well be that the German Camp Administration would be replaced by something much tougher. Did I desire that? I said: "Heaven forbid." He then suggested that the set should be handed to him and he gave me his word that it would be returned as soon as was prudent. I contacted Frank Stroobant. I did not —I did not dare—disclose that I proposed to hand it to the Germans. After much hesitation on the part of his colleagues, the set was placed on my bed and I took it to the Sonderführer who locked it in his cupboard which already contained, by previous arrangement between us, the Union Jack to which I refer later.

Within a day or so, the Bavarian Criminal Police (the Cripo) descended on us in force. Their personal search of internees and detailed search of the camp, in the course of which they threw the entire contents of all our lockers on the floor, made Ertl's previous effort look like a game of blind man's buff. It seems that they were looking for firearms which, it was rumoured in the village, we had in some quantity. They found none for the simple reason that we had none. On the conclusion of their activities, they held a conference in the Sonderführer's room little dreaming that, within feet of them, there reposed an object the discovery of which would undoubtedly have amply comforted them for the blank they had drawn in other directions. Within forty-eight hours, the wireless was back in our possession and Frank Stroobant resumed his nightly labours.

A day or so before we were liberated by the American Army, the German General commanding all P.O.W. and Internment Camps in our area, all of which except ours were already in American hands, came to Laufen to await the arrival of and surrender to the American Army. He sent for me and said: "It is only a matter of hours before you are liberated; I wish to alleviate your conditions if you will indicate what you wish." Utter chaos would have resulted had our gates been thrown open and our people freed to wander at will and I could think of nothing else that we lacked and he could provide. I told him so and left him. Within minutes it occurred to me how splendid it would be to get the B.B.C. openly over the loudspeaker. I went back and he at once gave orders accordingly. I went straight to the canteen and I was soon listening to the B.B.C. and had the unspeakable joy of hearing almost immediately that Churchill had just told the House of Commons that "tomorrow our dear Channel Islands will be free." It is a tribute to what Frank Stroobant had been doing for us for so long that it only occurred to me belatedly to make my request to the German General.

Early in 1945 (I am now unable to fix the date accurately) there arrived in our camp one Sunday evening a number of British officers together with General Bor Komorowski (of Warsaw fame who died recently) and his Polish H.Q. staff. I was allowed by the Commandant to talk to them and provide them with coffee. Among the British officers were Lord Lascelles (now the Earl of Harewood), the eldest son of H.R.H. the late Princess Royal; the Master of Elphinstone, a close relative of H.M. The Queen Mother, and Giles Romilly, related to Lady Churchill; and with them was Lieut. Winant, the son of the American Ambassador to the Court of St. James. They were in transit from Colditz to an unknown destination and were gravely concerned as to their fate. It was believed that the intention was to use them as hostages for Hitler's personal safety and that he was contemplating a last desperate stand in the Bavarian mountains. It may be that the rumour referred to in "One Man's War" that the Gestapo contemplated herding us into the cellars of the schloss and gassing us (of which I had never previously heard) was merely a variant and expansion of what was rumoured about the fate of these officers.

They went on to Tittmoning from whence Romilly made a spectacular escape and reached the American lines. The others hid in a vast disused chimney for days and the Germans thought they had escaped, too. I know our Commandant expected to lose his head as a result of it. Then they were brought back to Laufen where a P.O.W. camp in miniature was set up inside our schloss, they being separated from us by barbed wire and specially built masonry walls. They were guarded by a detachment of Luftwaffe commanded by an English-speaking Captain.

One Sunday afternoon news reached me that they were leaving at first light on the morrow. Deeply troubled concerning them, I approached the Luftwaffe officer and urged him to tell me their destination. I was proposing to contact the Protecting Power about them. I needn't have bothered for I have always understood that they knew already and that their representative arrived at the destination as soon as the officers did. In reply to my request, the officer said: "Obviously, you have information you ought not to have. I will not lie to you, we are leaving tomorrow but it is as much as my head is worth to tell you where we are going. If it will reassure you, I will tell you this: I have orders from my general that on no account are these officers to fall into the hands of the S.S. or the Gestapo and my men and I will die to the last man before that happens." He appeared to be absolutely sincere.

It seemed to us likely that the Russians would reach us before the Americans could and I was most anxious to have a large Union Jack to fly over our schloss for our protection if that happened. I tried vainly to obtain one first from Guernsey and then from England. Undeterred, I then got Padre Gerhold to paint one on a large linen sheet which had once been part of the hospital stores at Fort George, Guernsey. He could only get hold of water colours but, within those limitations, made an excellent job. It covered the coffin of ex-C.P.O. Dunkley, R.N., at his funeral in Laufen Cemetery on November 28th, 1944. Until needed, it was kept in the Sonderführer's cupboard. When American tanks rumbled into our village in the early afternoon of May 4th, 1945, it was displayed at our most prominent window. The effect was dramatic: the column halted and an American officer came to investigate. We were free. That flag flew proudly over our schloss for many days until, alas, the rains came and gradually obliterated its colours. Before that happened, it had attracted to us many escaping British prisoners of war, one party of whom, I remember, arrived in a German staff car fitted with inch-thick bullet-proof glass.

I have paid tribute to Frank Stroobant. There were many others whose devotion to duty was an inspiration, more than I have space to mention here. But I remember with particular gratitude Padre Gerhold (now Canon Gerhold, Rector of St. Pierre du Bois, Guernsey); Padre Flint of the Methodist Church and Brigadier Best of the Salvation Army; Wynne Sayer, our principal news-reader; "Postmaster" Boalch; our Red Cross workers, Ayres and Cranch; my Deputy Camp Seniors, Joe Eveson, Don Campbell and Len Collins; Cookson, who worked devotedly in the Revier (camp hospital); Ferguson, our chief cook for so long; Savage, Cooper and the others who did so much for education in the camp and our very able Jewish doctor, Oshek. I should be lacking in gratitude if I failed to remember the German Commandant, Oberst Kochenberger, and our dear old German Camp doctor, Dr. Schickehofer. He said to me once: "I am a Christian, I treat Jew and Gentile alike" and, when typhus broke out among the wretched, emaciated survivors from the concentration camp at Regensburg who reached our village, he told me: "I go now to take charge of the typhus hospital; it will be a good end." I am glad to say that, for him, it was not the end; indeed, when last I heard of him, he, a confirmed bachelor, was happily married.

CHAPTER I

A DECISION TO BE TAKEN

NATURALLY WE WERE shocked by the German defeat of
Poland; naturally we regretted the outbreak of War between
England and Hitler's Nazis; but apart from shock and regret
what was happening in Europe in the autumn of 1939 seemed
of little concern to us, secure in our snug, self-satisfied
island of Guernsey in the Channel Islands. Why, indeed,
should the machines of war and the machinations of poli-
ticians have anything to do with us? We were too small,
too easy to isolate to attract the attention of possible invaders.
Besides, the great armies of France and the whole might of
the Maginot Line lay between us and England's enemy. Of
course, we were safe!

So, though we might keep an eye on events, it was only
to satisfy our general curiosity. We liked to know what
was going on in our neighbour's back-yard, and for us,
Europe between the Atlantic and the Rhine was our back-
yard.

Even if we had not been so sure of ourselves, we might
have been encouraged to behave exactly as we did by the
stagnation of the " phoney " war. Did England really mean
to fight Germany; did Hitler, indeed, mean to fight England?
Any doubts we might have entertained had a legitimate basis
in the events of September 1939 to May 1940.

But if I say that we felt aloof from all that was happening, we were not entirely untouched by the rumblings of
the giants. For example, a black-out was imposed on us,
and A.R.P. wardens were appointed. It was no joke to patrol
the streets in pouring rain with no street lighting. It was
even less of a joke when the cost of special blinds and curtains
appeared an unnecessary expense, and our wanderings in the
dark streets so much waste of time.

When at last the Nazi war-machine began to streak
westwards with lightning speed, and the enemy came near
to us, then we dithered. Like hundreds, even thousands of
others, I did not know what to do.

13

Firstly, we were advised to register. Then we were told that an evacuation of the total population of the Island to England was certain. Next we heard, on reliable authority, that a wholesale evacuation would not take place; and some notices were displayed urging the people not to abandon the Island. But the notices did not help us, for some were official and the rest were not, and between the two the ordinary man got himself into a shocking tangle.

At one moment I almost gave my business away; it was not worth much in those days. But the next moment I met a man who assured me that the Germans would not waste their time or their troops in Guernsey. Passing on down the street I encountered friends as puzzled as I, who asked me what I thought. I could not tell them, because I did not know what to think myself. As I left them, another man came running up shouting that total evacuation had been decided upon.

I went home in complete bewilderment and switched on the wireless. The news from Broadcasting House provided no solution to my problem. Britain was struggling to rescue her valiant forces from the Dunkirk beaches, and seemed faced herself with the possibility of German invasion.

At last I came to myself, I would never find the answer by seeking advice from friends, neighbours or officials. I must make my own decisions!

Once having settled that in my mind, I determined that having set myself on a course, I would not turn aside from it. France was out of the fight, or would be very soon. Only a miracle could save her, but would a Joan of Arc appear? Her fall would bring the Germans to within twenty miles of us, and would they really allow the British to have potential basis within twenty miles of them? I thought not.

By this time the Island authorities had arranged an evacuation scheme for those who felt that their duty lay on the mainland. It seemed to me that if my wife and baby daughter were safely in England I should be able to follow them more easily on my own if it appeared that the Germans did intend to visit us.

I promised my wife I would follow. I felt sure that the call would come for all men of military age to evacuate to the mainland.

Assembly points had been arranged and would-be evacuees were warned to be ready to move at a moment's notice. Waiting for orders, we were worried, restless, on edge; but we hoped in our hearts that our parting would be short, that the emergency would be called off, and that normal life would return to us.

I remember wondering, at one moment, whether I had done the right thing in burdening my wife not only with the responsibility of her own existence but with that of our little girl as well. In sending them off like this, was I shirking my own responsibilities? If the Germans were to invade our Motherland, was I not sending them possibly into much greater danger? If they were going, ought not I to go as well so that if we had to struggle to carry on, we would all struggle together?

But other arguments told me that England meant safety. The islands might be overrun, but England would never allow Hitler to land; and I could not tear up all my roots in Guernsey — the roots from which my livelihood sprang — just like that, and go hurrying to England, from which we might be able to return in a few weeks — if Hitler decided the Channel Islands were beneath his notice — and then find my business gone and have to start again.

Nevertheless, it was difficult to have to be resolute in this decision, and I followed the bus carrying them down to the harbour numb in my mind.

The harbour was filled with shipping for the evacuation. Some ships had come straight from fulfilling their errands of mercy at Dunkirk to undertake another here. Their decks still bore the marks of what they had gone through.

Crowds, naturally, had gathered at the approaches to the harbour, and to avoid the confusion of fond farewells, barricades had been erected and only essential personnel and those who were to go were allowed inside them. I did not know this, and to bolster my own and my wife's morale I had not said my proper farewells at home.

When the buses had passed the barrier, I approached a constable on duty and told him I had urgent business in the harbour. To support this, while I spoke to him, I kept the engine of my van running. He may have believed me or he may not, but he let me through. His kindness, however, availed me nothing, for by the time I arrived my wife and baby were on board and all we could do was to wave forlornly to one another.

I shall probably be misunderstood when I say this, but when I noticed the kiosk on the jetty was closed I could hardly believe my eyes, and I thought at once of the needs of the evacuees and of the dockers and others, who had worked for hours without a break.

Realising that I should now never be able to say good-bye properly to my wife, I decided on the spur of the moment that I must try to do something about the kiosk. So I went in search of the man who could give me permission. I found him, together with another official in his office at the landside end of the jetty, and when I asked for authority to force a window of the kiosk and open it for service, he said: " Good for you, laddie! Go to it! "

They were words which I shall always remember, for they had consequences which were serious for me.

Running back to my van, I drove quickly to my main shop, collected staff and stock, and returned as quickly as I could to the kiosk. I personally forced a window and climbed through.

Before I opened the door to my staff I made a quick inventory of what was already in the kiosk, folded the paper and put it carefully in my pocket. Then I opened up to my staff and in a short time they were supplying the long-felt needs of hunger and thirst or the craving for a smoke of those who were selflessly helping their fellow islanders to safety.

When I had seen that all was going well, I made one more attempt to see my wife but I was not successful. When at last their ship moved away from the quay I waved to it in the hope that my family would notice. I could not see them as they were below decks. It was 10 months before I heard that they were safe and well.

You may guess my feelings during those months. The Germans had occupied the islands and all contact with England was cut. In the near-panic of the last days before the evacuation I had failed to make adequate financial arrangements for my wife and child in England and now could do nothing for them. I had given her what ready cash I had but it was not much. When, after 10 months, Red Cross messages did begin to trickle through from England, they were restricted to half-a-dozen words and could only say: " Safe and well. Love."

But my wife is a resourceful woman. She was not in England long before, preferring to make her own way without having to rely on Public Assistance, she had found accommodation for herself and the child, and her aged parents. Then, with a roof over their heads, she went in search of work and was given a job in a municipal office, where she developed friendships on which she looks back today with deep pleasure.

When a catastrophe such as this overtakes one, it is not of personal belongings that one thinks. The welfare of loved ones blots out everything else; and ignorance of what is happening to them and how they are faring fills one with constant, gnawing anxiety.

It was as bad for those who went as for those who stayed behind. Nor were we the only ones who suffered in this way. There were thousands and thousands who were sharing our deep anxiety, though this knowldege did little to help. For us who did stay there was a faint consolation; at least our loved ones were safe in England.

When the last ship had gone, life on the island returned to a sort of uneasy normality. It went on in this way while the French gradually rolled further and further back under the pressure of the Panzers and sheer weight of opposing infantry. As we heard the hourly worsening news we felt that we might soon have new experiences to meet. But it was a tremendous shock, all the same, when the Germans sent aircraft to attack us, and in their one and only raid on Guernsey killed 29 Guernseymen. The futility of the raid and the comparatively heavy casualties brought us face to face with stark reality, and I do not suppose there was one among us who did not thank God for this sign that we had done the right thing in sending our families away.

But before the Germans were to follow up their raid with a landing, I was to have a shock of another kind.

When I had returned to our empty house I had made up my mind that for as long as I was allowed by circumstances, I would carry on with my business as normally as possible. In my everyday goings and comings, therefore, I met many people and I do not recall anyone who had heard about it who did not compliment me on the opening of the kiosk in the harbour during the evacuation.

My dismay may be judged, therefore, when one morning Police Inspector F. Banneville called on me and served me with a summons to appear before the Magistrate's Court next day on a charge of " breaking into and entering the kiosk at the New Jetty."

When I had recovered my speech, I asked for clarification of the charge and learned that it had been lodged by the owner of the kiosk, who had been in the island all the time but had considered it unnecessary to provide a service for the hard-worked dockers and officials doing their utmost to save our families.

But when I thought it over and remembered that I had the permission of a States' official — the competent authority, as I thought — to do what I did, I felt confident that the outcome would be in my favour.

Once again, I was due for another shock! When the official was questioned in Court he stated blandly that he could not remember having given me permission and could not even remember my going to his office. As a result, the Acting Magistrate, Jurat Quertier Le Pelley, found the charge proven and bound me over for a year and a day.

I am still unhappy when I think back to this black mark which was put against my name. All I had wanted to do was to help; and I believe I did help. Besides, I sold only my own goods. The owners could check by the inventory I had made, and which was produced in Court.

CHAPTER II

UNDER THE JACKBOOT

Several books have been written about the German Occupation of the Channel Islands, and it is not my intention to go over the well-worn path of events, except to say that the first Nazis arrived in Guernsey on Sunday, June 30th, 1940, and that the first liberating British soldier stepped ashore on Wednesday, May 9th, 1945. The experience of these five years must appear, within the framework of general events, different to each individual. Some remember chiefly the acquisition or loss of a bicycle; or the barter system which had to be introduced, though unofficially, when the stocks in the shops ran out and were not renewed; or hiding a pig from the Germans; or the sight of human beings herded like cattle to forced labour, building the immense fortifications the Germans were erecting all around the island; or the emotion with which one heard the story of the forced-labourer who, seeing a little child, broke ranks, ran over to her, picked her up in his arms and showered her with kisses; or listening, illicitly, to the B.B.C.; or the hardship of German restrictions on movements.

From my own point of view, the latter loomed large, and never more so than in the summer months. May to September have always meant hours of lazing on the beaches, swimming and playing cricket. The bays and the beaches were now forbidden to us, cut off from us by formidable barbed wire and gun emplacements. The sand playgrounds of the children were cut up with tank-traps and lethal with mine-fields. The cliff paths, always so popular with young couples, were out of bounds.

Everywhere you looked there were warning notices and there was at least one German word in all our vocabularies: VERBOTEN.

Guernsey was certainly not the same, but the parts of it which remained free to us reminded us of times past and of future hopes.

They could not change the seasons. The spring flowers could not be delayed because of barbed wire, and because spring is more than a season of hope, each spring cheered us on into believing that this summer would be the last our uninvited guests would spend with us. Then, as summer changed into autumn and we all scoured the island for twigs, logs, pine cones and anything else that would burn, we would sit down by our almost empty grates and remember the dinners, the parties, the hand-overs, the new dresses, the dances and wonder what our friends who had shared the winter social round with us were doing now.

We had more time now for thinking than we had ever had before in our lives, and new thoughts came to us, and a new appreciation of our heritage — the beauties of our island we had grown so accustomed to accept that we scarcely noticed them. Now, deprived of many of them, we realised what they meant to us for the first time. Nor were the natural beauties alone made more precious to us. The bequests of our ancestors took on a new value. Castle Cornet we had seen as an ancient stronghold. Now, it was a symbol of our island's strength, though over it flew the Swastika, when, before, the Union Jack had flown almost without our noticing it. Then, too, there had been the visitors who had come to see us every year in their thousands. Without them, how could the summer be the same? And, how could it be the same when the glasshouses were no longer crammed to the doors with tomatoes, and the long lines of lorries no longer queued at the harbour to load millions of chips of our island's chief produce on ships for England? Instead, our harbour, one of the finest of its size, now sheltered enemy craft, from supply ships to submarines. The Pool was empty, too, of the little boats in which we had whiled away pleasant afternoons of freedom in the waters between the islands; and the fisherman no longer went freely out to let down his lobster pots.

On Saturday afternoons and evenings the High Street of St. Peter Port had always been so thick with people that it was scarcely possible to move. Now it was well-nigh deserted. What was the good of coming to buy from shops that had nothing to sell?

And, of course, there was always the thought of our loved ones from whom we were separated.

With others, I would often stand for hours at a time at a northern point of the island and look out towards the Casquets, and the lighthouse, just discernible on the horizon, which had guided the ships past the dangerous rocks, speeding them on their way to England. Now, there was no light; there were no ships. England might as well have not existed for us. Yet in England were our wives and daughters, sons, mothers and fathers.

If we wondered what was happening in England, we wondered, too, what was happening in France, and in Herm and Sark. And how were our cousins in Jersey making out under the jackboot? Against our 20,000 they had evacuated only a few thousand, so if we found living difficult, what must it be for them?

Was Jersey's geographical position to their advantage or disadvantage, I wondered? With that additional 20 miles of sea to be covered and their close proximity to the French coast, the risk of taking the evacuation ships into St. Helier must have been a much greater one than using St. Peter Port Harbour. Possibly that accounts for the comparative size of the evacuation.

On the other hand I felt that being so near to France would enable them to be supplied more easily and the possibility of trading greater than for Guernsey, which is the farthest west of the Channel Islands.

All these were new thoughts for us. In peace we had thought only of ourselves. Now the fate of others had become a daily topic of conversation.

From those separated from us our thoughts would turn to those still with us. Old So-and-So was taking things badly. He was trying to live on his own and keep his little home together, but the strain was proving too much for him. Old Jack, though, was making the best of a bad job. Someone had seen him out with a " bit of skirt." Disloyal? Unfaithful? Who were we to judge, even if our inclinations in these things did not make them a necessity? But when that " bit of skirt " deserted old Jack and turned " Jerry bag," as we called it, we thought it a great shame; then, as like as not, our new tolerance got the better of us and if we did not know the excuse we invented one — was she imitating Mata Hari? If she only wanted more to eat, were we to blame her?

Few people bothered to listen to the German news, but quite a number tuned in nightly to Lord Haw-Haw just to be able to ridicule his harangue at first hand. Even fewer people visited the cinema, where only German films were shown. The handful who did go reported excellent entertainment, but, after all, we had our pride. Proudly we would suffer at the hands of Germans; but it would be shameful to enjoy ourselves by collaborating with them.

To me and others like me who were devoted to sport, the news that our beautiful Elizabeth College cricket ground was scheduled to come under the plough was one of the hardest blows we had to take. For some time now it had been used as a timber yard and deep furrows had been cut into the priceless turf, but not so badly that it could not be repaired. But if the turf were to be destroyed completely . . . ! It did not bear thinking of; and many of us would have preferred to go hungry than to eat the produce of this sacred turf.

Assuredly, we were in a minority. To the average householder what was to sportsmen a tragedy was nothing compared with the fact that at any time of the day or night an order might be received to quit their home which was to be requisitioned for some branch or other of Hitler's organisation. Families were thrown into each other's arms whether they liked it or not. Often it happened that no sooner had the evicted found sanctuary than the sanctuary itself was seized. Those who thus suffered bore their troubles with dignity, but after two or possibly three upheavals, their regard for the German Führer really touched bottom.

The switch from driving on the left side of the road to the right did not cause many of us inconvenience, as there were very few who were not compelled to walk by reason of the confiscation of private means of transport and the failure to provide adequate buses. But it did remind us that we were now a part of the Continent, for the first time for nearly a thousand years, though we hoped this new status would be very temporary.

As Occupation Marks appeared, so Guernsey and English money disappeared. Much of it did not fall into German hands but was stowed away in some secret place against the great day of Liberation. There were rare occasions, however, when a deal demanding "real" money came along. Then the hoards would be raided and the bargains struck.

One good thing resulted from the German stay with us. Several of our very dangerous corners vanished, and road widening schemes which had been under discussion by the States (our administration) since the accession of Queen Victoria to the throne of Great Britain were completed overnight. Though, at the time, there was sympathy for those who lost their land without compensation, the motorist, who forms a large percentage of the population, appreciates the improvements particularly now that traffic on the roads is heavier than pre-war.

Our standard of living in the Island had always been fairly high since the tomato industry had become our main source of income and perhaps we had been pampered in many respects. This was certainly true of what might be called the leisure time devoted to entertainment of a more intellectual nature. We had, for example, become used to first-rate repertory theatre and to music-hall artistes from England.

We might have turned to the radio partially to fill the gap created in this aspect of our lives by the Occupation, had not listening to the B.B.C., after being permitted for a period at the time that the allies were under pressure, eventually been forbidden. The German programmes in English were poor fare as far as entertainment value went, even if our patriotic urge had not placed a moral embargo on our listening to them.

But besides being denied the entertainment of films, radio and theatre, our leisure hours were now greatly increased on account of the almost complete standstill to which our working activities were brought. We realised that boredom can react against morale as nothing else can except hunger, and had to be cast about for some means of filling the long, vacant hours. Country walks were out of the question since, on the Occupation rations, they were too exhausting, though we found that it was possible to indulge in some sport without becoming too hungry.

Sport of all kinds, therefore, suddenly began to flourish and supporters increased considerably, possibly through lack of other entertainment. One-time players and youngsters who normally would have been unable to take an active interest in cricket and football, either because they lacked the flannels or shorts or equipment, or because they could not make the required grade, now found that they had the time and that cricket can be played as well in dungarees as in immaculate "whites". Soon the main problem was not wickets, balls, goalposts, regulation jerseys and shorts, but a lack of pitches.

As I have already said, the Germans soon cast envious eyes on our beautiful cricket-ground — if I seem to emphasize cricket more than any other sport, it is because I have always been a devotee — and had requisitioned part of it for a timber yard, and soon it was rumoured that they planned to plough up the rest. All lovers of the game felt compelled to rally to its defence, therefore, and we decided that one of the best ways of doing so was to keep it in constant use. This meant giving all those who wished to play an equal chance, even if they had to take the field in their underpants.

A rally was organised and attended by a truly great crowd, many of whom, I am sure, thought " short leg " to be a physical handicap. Though the Germans were even more ignorant of the game, they did see that the field was vital to the life of the island and for the pacification of the islanders, and they had second thoughts about using the plough.

Before the War, the class system in Guernsey had been highly organised. It was almost impossible either to step up, out of, or step down into a stratum that was not your own. During the Occupation there was a tremendous levelling in both directions, and though the problem of obtaining food was undoubtedly one cause of this, I like to think that "Le Sport" also played a highly important rôle. You found now that you were just a member of a team. No question was asked about your pedigree, nor whether you delivered groceries, bread or meat, nor whether your father had played poker with the Dalai Lama of Tibet. The main object was to keep the Germans off our ground, and if you could help, you were as welcome as any officer of State. And so we came to know one another better and, realising how easy it had been to misjudge, we revised many of our opinions.

Football also flourished and it was during the Occupation that Guernsey produced such outstanding players as Len Duquemin and Bill Whare, who, after it was all over, carried the island's good name into the professional ranks of First Division English football.

Other sports were also kept going, though a good deal of improvisation was called for. Indeed, our sporting activities caused much speculation among the Germans who, motivated completely by the principle of *Alles für den Krieg*, could not understand how we could be playing games and laughing when our country, in their view, but certainly not in ours, was on the verge of total defeat.

The normal procedure in ordinary times after a sporting engagement is to repair to the local pub and hold an inquest over the odd half-pint. The inquests were still held, though not very often stimulated by beer. As time went by, the publican had to ration his entirely inadequate supplies not only to regular customers but to greatly curtailed hours. But he played his part well, for not until after D-Day, when Guernsey was completely cut off from the outside world and the islanders were subjected to the greatest privations, did the pubs have to close altogether. Thanks to the efforts of the local buying commission, led by Raymond Falla, who periodically visited France, where they secured vital supplies of foodstuffs and deserve the gratitude of the whole population, allocations of brandy, liqueurs and white table wines were also generally forthcoming, even if good, honest ale was not, for though beer was obtainable in very limited quantities, it could best be described as " not very near beer," and closely resembled in appearance and taste our local quarry water.

If we rose to the occasion for outdoor entertainments, we were no less active when presented with long winter evenings to fill. For this we turned to the stage, and in our amateur way strove to replace those who had professionally diverted us in saner and more expansive times. I am proud to have been connected with the wartime theatre in Guernsey, as President of the Guernsey Co-Optimists, for though we might bewilder the Germans with our accent on sports, the stage as a propaganda weapon was not unknown to them, and the frustrations of their strict censorship and our lack of equipment seemed to make our efforts that much more worthwhile. We sought for no personal reward beyond bringing some relief to our fellows, contributing to local charities, and I must say that they rallied to us in a most encouraging way, filling all "houses" with enthusiastic audiences.

As in sport, so in the theatre, we recognised the value of the competitive spirit. At least three companies were formed and besides vying with each other to produce the outstanding performances, they were able to operate the theatre with almost unbroken continuity. The great majority of our shows could claim to have three objectives. First, we sought to provide with amateur talent a performance which would at least equal, but we hoped surpass, any previous productions; second, we aimed at attracting the maximum audiences so that the charities we supported might benefit by the largest possible sums; and, third, to take our audiences "out of themselves" for an hour or two and make them forget the harsh realities.

This final aim was considered by many to be our outstanding contribution — and perhaps it was. But besides helping in these various ways those who patronised us, there was yet another value accruing from our efforts, this time connected with the players themselves. This was the occupation of leisure time demanded by rehearsals and performances. So greatly was this esteemed that the three companies were overwhelmed by applications from those who wished to join them, either as actors or in any capacity behind the scenes or in the front of the house.

For our charities, we had not far to search. The conditions of the Occupation brought the standard of life of the average worker and those on small fixed incomes to danger point. I have records of our company which show that the plays produced by it provided no less than £1,000 towards the relief of the worst hit by the Occupation.

There was a marked increase in Church and Chapel congregations. The casual worshipper would creep into a back pew. I was one of them.

Though our personal lives were affected to an extent and in ways which it had never occurred to us would be possible, it can be seen, from what I have just stated, that we were resilient enough to be able to adapt ourselves to the new conditions. There was, however, one aspect of island life about which we could do nothing.

Within a short time of the arrival of the Germans, the island's trade, to all intents and purposes, came to a standstill. To begin with there was a situation in which panic was the main element.

It did not take long to realise that now we were cut off from England we should be unable to replenish our stocks. A result of this realisation was a mad rush of buying and selling. The people with money went from shop to shop buying up whatever they could find, whether they needed it or not. Possibly there lay behind their actions the idea that since money would soon have no value, it would be safer to turn it into goods. Coupled with this, of course, was the certainty that when the shops were empty all goods would appreciate in value. This panic buying did not affect anything controlled by the Essential Commodities Committee who had exercised great foresight in their rationing schemes.

Some of the tradesmen, foreseeing what would happen, countered by putting stock out of sight so that they might be able to supply regular customers; the tradesmen themselves, however, cannot be acquitted of the charge of " having an eye to the future" and of hoarding stock so that they might benefit from the inflated prices of the shortage. Very quickly, trading assumed an under-the-counter aspect, but whether these tactics were legitimate or not, there were certain types of business which could not avoid failing. Particularly was this the case when the amount of stock held was small. As the Occupation advanced, therefore, several shops were operating purely on barter trading. In some cases this barter trading was merely a cover for Black Market dealings, which did not ease the position at all.

In all cases of shortage or rising prices, it is the people living on small fixed incomes, such as old age pensioners, who are the first to suffer. Apart from their essential rations, which were strictly and fairly controlled by the various States' committees, these people were soon suffering badly. As this was an inevitable outcome of conditions, so it was inevitable that those with money or with goods for barter did not suffer so much. The German soldier was always willing to buy something to take home to the family when he went on leave. Often he would barter, and in this way became the source of little luxuries and extras such as cigarettes, from which the more unfortunate were completely cut off.

Yet even out of this disaster some good came. The pre-war nine-hour day, with 15 hours on Saturday for shop-workers, by becoming a wartime 20-hour week, paved the way for post-war working conditions which could only bene-fit the worker, for they made it possible to introduce reason-able hours, wage minima and other conditions of employ-ment more easily than might otherwise have been the case.

Before the War, as now, our island economy was based on our tomato production. With our main market cut off, the bulk of the tomato crop for 1940 was left to waste or be given away, and in subsequent years, only sufficient for home consumption was grown. This collapse of our major industry also had its effect not only on the island economy, but on the lives of the large numbers of islanders who made their living either as growers or workers in the greenhouses.

Almost from the earliest days of the Occupation the main concern of everyone was to obtain sufficient food to sustain life. A hungry people can be a dangerous people; dangerous, not only to themselves, for when the body is deprived of substance the mind becomes sick and the stan-dard of morale deteriorates. It says much for the moral strength of the Guernseyman that he managed to maintain a fairly high standard of morals and morale. The least sign of hostility on the part of the Guernsey public could result in collective punitive action by the Germans. Resistance, therefore, could only be shown in passive form, but no occa-sion on which their true feelings might be expressed was ever missed by the islanders. Perhaps the most inspiring example of this was at the time that 19 bodies of British sailors drowned when H.M.S. *Charybdis* was mined and sunk, were washed ashore and accorded a military funeral by the Germans. Scarcely an islander was absent from the service, and no fewer than 721 wreaths were sent.

I suppose if the Guernseyman had not been what he is —stubborn and proud—he might have fared better than he did. I do not mean in the matter of food—we were a conquered people and could only expect just to be kept alive by our captors—but in the conditions of life.

The arrival and hiding of two British military agents, Lieut. J. M. Symes and Lieut. H. F. Nicolle, both Guernseymen, was merely the culmination of a series of acts of resistance which brought down on us the wrath of the Germans. But this incident seemed to convince the Germans that we should never learn to accept them as they had hoped and had set themselves out to achieve. So they merely gave up trying to win us over; instead, they adopted a programme which would give us real cause to hate; a programme in which I was destined to be involved.

CHAPTER III

HOME FROM HOME

My FATHER HAD BEEN born in Guernsey but had moved to England as a young man. Towards the end of the First World War he returned to the island, where he died shortly afterwards. I was then 10 years old.

Due, possibly, to my so-called Cockney accent and my inability to understand the *patois* spoken by some of my new schoolmates at the States Intermediate School, I took some time to settle down in my fresh surroundings, but eventually found my niche, and made friends.

At school I was able to maintain a steady position just off the bottom of the class, and this made me content to concentrate more on my physical than on my mental development. This, I may say, I achieved in the face of strong opposition from my various masters, who seemed to take a perverse delight in attempting to " make something out of me " academically.

But they were on a sticky wicket. I knew my own limitations, set my own goals accordingly and would not let myself be deflected from attaining them by any well-wishing master who thought otherwise. I was so successful that the closing phases of my school career I regard as entirely satisfactory. I was captain of this, champion of that and, greatest achievement of all, winner of the most coveted prize—" For the best-liked boy in the school "—an award made by the ballot of the whole school.

I must confess that this award was responsible for leading me into a misconception. I firmly believed that the headmaster, Mr. F. E. Fulford, would one day send for me and address me in some such terms as the following: " Stroobant, you're a jolly fine chap. Would you like a commission in the Army or the Navy? Or should I recommend you for training to become a professional cricketer or for any other form of sport? "

This was my day-dream, and it was soon to be rudely shattered. The headmaster did send for me, but his words were not laudatory.

"You're a fine, useless lad," he said. "Your scholastic achievements are subnormal and, in fact, I advise you to learn some trade at once before you are too old to be accepted for an apprenticeship."

When eventually I plucked up the courage to tell my mother of this interview, she had to agree. As it was not difficult to become apprenticed to a carpenter, W. J. Hall, of Vauvert, that was the trade we chose. From the moment I started to learn my trade, I took an intense dislike to it. Perhaps the first job I was sent out on was in some way responsible for this. I had to help to put a corpse in a coffin made by my master, and as I lifted the head the corpse let forth a loud groan (caused by air left in the lungs) and it was some time before I recovered from the shock.

But though I was unmercifully ragged by my fellow apprentices and many untoward incidents overtook me, partly due to many late nights, I stuck at it until I overslept one day and did not wake until 4 p.m. By this time I had lost my mother as well as my father and was being brought up by two aunts who did not approve of the late hours I kept. They had warned me that if I did not get up more promptly in the mornings they would leave me to my own devices and were as good as their word.

I decided to lose a day's pay and plead an emergency next morning. I fear, however, that when I did arrive I was "late again" and after an acrimonious scene with my employers moved to another job.

A variety of employment followed during the next two or three years. At twenty-one I should inherit my father's estate, so I cast about to find something which would keep me occupied when that time came, without my having to work hard. Taking stock of possible ways of doing this, I came to the conclusion that anyone in business had a "snip". In fact, it seemed to me then that all they had to do was to stand behind a counter and give change. They might have to make general conversation with a few old ladies, but if they could talk about local events and count up to 12, it should be dead easy.

The next thing was to decide on the type of business and when to set up shop. A tobacconist's and confectioner's, I thought, should bring my friends rallying round, so I looked about for a site, found one in Church Street, set myself up, and took a partner, W. H. Symes, to look after the shop while I was otherwise engaged.

This was the beginning of a business career in which I am still engaged. In ignorance I did many foolish things, and there were some very unpleasant moments. I branched out in all directions, which included subsidiary ventures quite unconnected with my main interest. Most of these swallowed up money at an alarming rate.

At the bleakest moment I entered what is called the "desirable state of matrimony" and it was this which gave me the courage and energy to pull myself out of my difficulties. Though it meant a considerable amount of hard work — I often laughed to myself when I recalled that I had gone into business to avoid hard work — the incentive to make good was there, and it was the right one. Gradually things took a turn for the better.

During these activities I had not neglected sport. I played a good deal of cricket and became interested in water-polo and boxing; I wrecked a gliding club's only glider and I joined the Royal Guernsey Militia. It was a full life but a happy, zestful, interesting and worthwhile life.

With the Occupation my business, of course, took a blow from which it could never hope to recover while the Germans were still with us. Though I may have learned a good deal more than I knew when I first started, I was, however, still prepared to "try anything once" and when I realised the facts of my situation, I gaily launched out into any business activity which would keep me occupied so long as resources lasted. One such activity was a café which I called The Home from Home.

Just before the war I had operated a business in a building situated on the sea-front, overlooking St. Peter Port harbour. It was a large two-storeyed building and only the ground-floor was occupied by my business. On the first floor there were two large rooms roughly 60 feet by 30 feet and 15 feet by 30 feet, which I decided were ideally suitable for a restaurant and kitchen. They had a good entrance and staircase and commanded an excellent view of all that was happening in the harbour and the roads bordering the harbour.

Although I might have laughed rudely had the idea been put to me, because it had come to me I found it very acceptable. Besides, the need for such an establishment was considerable since several of the usual cafés and restaurants had been closed by a variety of events during the period of near-panic. I think I am right in saying that in the town area alone no fewer than seven cafés had shut their doors.

Once having decided on the venture soon after my family had evacuated, I fully realised that failing compulsory evacuation, I should have to stay in the island should the Germans actually come. That I was prepared to risk; so I secured the upstairs rooms for a very reasonable figure —due to the times! and within 48 hours of moving in I was advertising the Home from Home in the local press.

The Home from Home quickly achieved a reputation, particularly among the many grass-widowers who now had to fend for themselves. They formed a regular clientèle.

To begin with, stocks of essential foods were adequate. When I had made my decision I had contacted the Custodian of Vacated Properties, Mr. C. E. Gicquel, and asked for his approval, which he gave with the assurance that I should have every possible assistance. The Essential Commodities Committee, which had controlled our rationing since the beginning of the War, granted me a favourable allocation of soap powders, powdered milk, tinned goods and dried fruit, but it was surprising how quickly supplies were used and I was always on the look-out for what I called day-to-day stock.

As an example of this there was the little matter of eggs which cropped up after the Germans had landed. I heard one day that a quantity of eggs could be collected for cash from a country address at the Gouffre. As one of my chief problems was transport I had bought a tradesman's bicycle with baskets fore and aft which, though it had rendered fine service to its previous owners for many years, was still sound in wind and limb.

As soon as I heard about the eggs, I took Aunt Agatha, as I had christened the bicycle, and rode out into the country. The way was nearly all uphill and there was quite a strong headwind blowing, but I consoled myself with the thought of the advantage both would give me on the return journey.

It took me over two hours to reach my destination and I was then faced with a flat denial that the story I had heard was true. But when I explained why I wanted the eggs and gave an assurance that only " our own people " would benefit from them, the seller ushered me secretly into his sanctum, where we negotiated a price for 300 eggs.

Having promised not to reveal the source of my supplies to anyone, I packed the eggs, already done up in a fashion which the vendor assured me was absolutely safe, fore and aft on " Aunt Agatha " and set out for town. Reaching the crest of the first incline, I decided to try a steady free-wheel down but at that very moment noticed yellow egg yolk seeping through the front basket. Gradually the trickle became a steady stream, and soon my trousers were wet with egg slime. Nor was this the total of my troubles, for the head-on wind on the way out had now completely changed round and was once more meeting me head on, at almost gale force.

Deciding that my most economical course was to get home as quickly as possible, I rode on, head down in the gale. Within a few minutes the paper covering the eggs in front of the basket blew up into my face, with the result that I was now a sticky mess from head to foot. I was beginning to wonder whether there would be one sound egg at the end of my journey.

It was with an immense sigh of relief that I eventually drew up before The Home from Home, and called for help. Though I did not feel at all amused, I must have looked very funny, for I was greeted with loud laughter and cheers.

The first task was to unload the eggs and find out what the damage was. I seem to remember that 78 eggs were a total loss, a further 60 cracked but usable in scrambled eggs and omelettes, while the rest were intact and helped subsequently to enhance The Home from Home's reputation for quality.

It was, in fact, the quality of our food which brought me into my head-on clash with the German authorities. I had pledged to myself that The Home from Home should be just that for our own people only, and when the first German soldiers and sailors began to come in, firmly but politely, I refused to serve them. This went on for about a month and then, one day, an officer from the Feldkommandantur called and demanded my reasons for excluding Germans from my café. I explained that I could get only sufficient supplies for my regular customers, and that anyway the soldiers had their own canteen facilities. This seemed to satisfy him and he went away, but in a short time he was back to warn me that if I did not admit Germans my café would be closed.

I had no alternative but to acquiesce and at once began adding bicarbonate of soda to each brew of tea to economise on the tea stock which I had been able to accumulate. I visited the Essential Commodities food store in St. Julian's House and bought everything I could lay hands on — soups, jam, soap and so on in catering packs; and I conceived a crafty idea.

Whilst at the store I was shown a quantity of large tinned hams which had " blown " and were about to be dumped as unfit for human consumption. On the spur of the moment I offered a price for the lot, provided I could take one tin with me first to experiment.

When the tin was opened, the ham stank to high heaven, but there were parts of it which were not too greatly discoloured. Naturally I could not offer it to my "regulars" but what about the Germans? I might even be able to carry out a little resistance, for I was sure that anyone eating it would immediately become *hors de combat* for many days.

The meat stank so much that my staff refused to handle it, so I took orders for it myself and served it. Having served my first customer, a German of gluttonous appearance, I retreated to watch the consequences, and was elated when he bellowed for more. At the earliest moment, I hurried back to the food store and bought the whole consignment.

It is quite clear to me that German stomachs are of a different calibre from our own. Perhaps they have a special lining, or special protective digestive juices which ours lack, but it is a fact that these cretinous Huns — many of them, on first arriving in Guernsey, had believed that they were in the Isle of Wight — seemed to thrive on this food which our officials, even in the face of direst shortage, had declared unfit for human consumption. Although I continued to serve it myself until supplies were exhausted, always on the look-out for groaning collapses, they tucked it away and came back for more without a single casualty.

About this time I formed a friendship which holds one of the happiest memories of the Occupation for me, and if he could have talked I believe this little mongrel terrier, whom I called Spot, owned by Mr. and Mrs. Harry Ferguson, of New Paris Street, would have voiced this opinion [See plate 1]. Actually he belonged to one of my staff, but he took such a liking to me that soon he was following me, wherever I went, spending the day at my side. Perhaps I ought to qualify this, for like the rest of the staff he found the " blown " ham too overpowering and when I was cutting it up in the cellar, he would retreat to the stairway and sit there until I had finished . When I went home to Osmond and Marion Le Lacheur's house in Doyle Road at the end of the day he would accompany me to my gate, and there we would have to say good-night, for there was already a dog in the family. His favourite task was to carry my empty bag for me on the way back from the Bank. Our companionship continued until I was forcibly moved on by our visitors, but when I returned after the Liberation I was delighted to find that Spot had escaped the fate of many domestic pets during the final dreadful months of the Occupation, when starvation, particularly among the enemy, led to the conversion of dogs and cats into sausage meat. I met Spot in the Arcade one day shortly after my return. Though he was aged and almost blind, I recognised him at once and called out to him. His immediate recognition gave me pleasure such as I shall never forget.

To return to the food problems which beset The Home from Home, among the greatest was to know what to use for fat for cooking, because early in the Occupation the essential foods were issued to householders only. It was one of the first problems to confront us, as a matter of fact.

Having little knowledge of the subject, I sought advice and then began to experiment myself. With liquid paraffin and olive oil I was successful, but unfortunately the stocks of these were soon used up and very soon I was reduced to considering motor oils and linseed oil.

I must confess that I had no idea about what would boil and what would not and as I had to work quickly, and personally did not care much for the idea of motor oil, I bought a sufficient quantity of linseed oil to give me an experimental deep-fry. As soon as the staff had gone home I began my experiment. I closed all the windows and poured my oil into an unused chip-fryer. Within a very short time I was reduced to semi-consciousness. The fumes were so over-powering that I had to tie a handkerchief over my nose and mouth, and not daring to open the door to the restaurant because of the terrible odour getting in there and staying, I threw open the windows. The pungent fumes billowed out into the street — and into the houses opposite, since the kitchen was on the Pollet land-side of the building, and I was soon the object of some extremely cutting remarks from their inhabitants. Fearing for the reputation of The Home from Home, which I thought might legitimately be mistaken for a tannery, I closed the windows again and decided to suffer in silence. My discomfort was rewarded by the achievement of my object. The oil came to the boil and I put a few chips into it. When I thought they must be done, I tried them and was almost done myself. Their taste was indescribable! Had I failed after all? At all events I could not make another attempt that night.

When I got home to Doyle Road the odour rising from my clothes betrayed me. I had to admit I smelt like a paint-shop. But out of our parleys came a glimmer of hope. I was advised to try putting an onion into the oil before boiling it up. In theory this should absorb both fumes and linseed taste.

Next evening I could hardly wait to begin my experiments again. Conditions were so much improved that even Spot came back into the kitchen; the previous night he had hidden himself as far from the kitchen as he could. To give myself a start I had forgone my tea. Although the chips had a definitely novel taste it was, I considered, a taste which could be acquired.

To make absolutely certain, I experimented once more the following night, and when the resulting chips had an almost normal flavour — or was I getting used to it? — I decided to lay in as much linseed oil as I could find. Some I bought, some I acquired by barter. It is surprising how human nature reacts to circumstances in which replacement of any goods is not possible. Few people could now have had any use for their linseed oil, yet they were most reluctant to part with it, simply because they would not be able to get any more. When, at last, I was sure that I had tapped all sources, I found myself the proud possessor of 70 gallons of valuable oil, which I stored safely under the staircase in a large cupboard.

Between the first experimental fry and the standard I was soon to reach there was a great difference. I am certain that very few of my customers had the faintest inkling of the oil their chips were fried in. For some time I took the precaution of making the first " fry " when the café was closed, for it was still a somewhat smelly operation, though the added onion did make the difference between its being unbearable and merely unpleasant.

As time went by, naturally, my use of the onions made serious in-roads into our small and previous stock. My cook, Edith Ferguson, and I had opposing views as to the value of the onions, she insisting that they were worth more as a flavouring in the utility dishes we were serving, whereas I was of the opinion that their fume-absorbent qualities were more precious. However, as cooks were not easy to come by, I gave in as gracefully as I could, and cast about for a substitute for the onion. Actually I found one more easily than I had ever dared to hope. A small block of wood — red deal proved the most satisfactory — did the job almost as well as the onion, and certainly well enough.

I had a cellar full of roots which was always a source of anxiety. As root vegetables age, so their edible value decreases and gives rise to more and more wastage, plus a distinctly unpleasant odour. Not only that, their cleaning and preparation took up an increasing number of man-hours, so that eventually I spent practically the whole of my time in the cellar together with the faithful Spot. The smell down there was overpowering until you got used to it, but even that I turned to advantage. If I had a caller I did not particularly wish to see, I received him in the cellar. Very quickly he discovered that he had another, more pressing, appointment.

I soon found that my stock of roots was in excess of the café's needs, and despite my constant pruning, deterioration was rapid. I offered some to friends and on Tuesday and Friday afternoons I had one hour's public sale at 3 p.m. When word got around the queue formed before 2 p.m.; usually I sold only the bruised stock after cutting out the rotted matter.

Among the regular customers were Mr. and Mrs. Godfrey Giffard, who did a splendid job looking after the poor at St. Barnabas' Mission. My intention had been to avoid wastage. For weighing, I used a personal weight machine on which a pound or so either way could easily happen, but after one dear old lady had weighed her purchases on her home scales, found short weight and lodged an official complaint I was advised to use proper scales, the cost of which was more than the total week's turnover; so I restricted sales to those who were prepared to come into the cellar — at the risk of getting asphyxiated — and collect their ration.

The week's great event was the Sunday afternoon tea hour, as there was little else to do. By opening time at 3.30 p.m. the queue was long and required control. When I opened the doors the rush was so great that it was not possible to close them again. However, by a mixture of force and persuasion the café was filled in a reasonably orderly manner and the customers were served with the delicious bi-carb-cum-tea beverage and whatever the menu could offer, which at that time was the choice between swede rissoles or limpet and parsnip fishcakes, served against a background of music by Stan Workman on the piano.

As the catering position deteriorated, so it became necessary to reduce the working hours of the staff. But every Sunday and holiday, wet or fine, I would take stock, and particularly of the oil. It was the latter which ran me into what might have been a serious mishap.

On August Bank Holiday, 1941, when I had gone over the rest of the stock, I unlocked the cupboard under the stairs where I kept the oil, and went inside, pulling the door shut after me. I made sure that the drums had not leaked, estimated the quantity I had left, and, satisfied, told myself that I could now enjoy the rest of the day, which was also my birthday.

With this thought, however, came the sudden realisation that the door of the cupboard was closed, that there was no means of opening it from the inside and that I was, therefore, a prisoner!

The only way of communicating with the outside world was through a small pane of glass above the doorway, which opened outward for about three inches. To reach it, I had to clamber on to boxes, shakily stacked below it. Opening the fanlight, I listened carefully for footsteps approaching along the pavement, which was about 20 feet away.

Each time I heard a sound I called out loudly, but for at least two hours I had no luck. At least one passer-by must have heard my calls, for he stopped, stepped back and looked at the café windows and then walked on.

By mid-day a note of desperation had crept into my voice. Then suddenly I managed to arrest the attention of a bespectacled youth. He hesitated, then approached the cupboard door for closer scrutiny. I called out for the details of my predicament to him, but it did not seem to register. was he a mute? When I repeated my difficulty, he answered in a foreign language and that immediately complicated matters for me. Would it be wise, I wondered, for me to throw out the key to him? He might walk off with it and my position would be worse than now.

But then he tried to open the door and I was certain I had found a friend. Putting my hand through the opening, I dropped the key to him and he quickly released me.

With the help of signs and the few words of German I could muster, and his smattering of French and English, I learned that he was Dutch, 18 years old, and sent to Guernsey for forced labour. He declined the money which I offered him but when I suggested a meal he accepted joyfully. So I opened one of my few remaining tins of pilchards and found some bread and one or two other scraps, and watched him eating hungrily. From further complicated conversation, I gathered that he was eager to learn English, and as I felt much indebted to him and believed that my own knowledge of our language might thereby be improved, I offered to help him. From then on he would come to see me at the café as often as he could and while he helped me clean up in the cellar, we talked English. He was an apt pupil, and it was not long before he was speaking reasonably fluently.

I have already mentioned that I had to allow Germans to come to the café. To give the soldiers their due, they caused no trouble, and I might have accepted them with good grace had I not always remembered that most of the food they ate could have been enjoyed by our own people. The Organisation Todt — the labour service — on the other hand, were a pestilential nuisance.

These men would always bring alcohol with them and though I refused to let them drink it on the premises, telling them so was very often like talking to a brick wall. As I could not throw my weight about with them, I just had to accept the situation.

There came a day, however, when I narrowly missed stopping a bottle with my head. This was bad enough, but worse was to come, for the bottle was followed by a table, which sailed across the café and landed in a showcase where all the glasses were kept. I suppose it should be mentioned that the violence was engendered by Stan Workman's spontaneous rendering of *"Hang Out the Washing on the Siegfried Line."* When peace was finally restored Stan was suspended from duty for 14 days after a solemn promise of no repeat effort.

When this gentleman eventually passed out and was carried away by his companions, I decided that I must act to prevent a repetition, otherwise I should soon have no staff left, and I should be serving drinks out of tin mugs. So at the earliest opportunity, I called at the Kommandantur, where I explained as forcibly as I could what had happened as a result of their ordering me to admit their men, and pointed out how impossible it was replacing breakages, as well as the risks of someone getting badly hurt. I demanded a firm order in official form and in writing which I could display, saying that the consumption of alcohol in The Home from Home was *strengst verboten*. This they gave me, and it proved very useful protection in the future.

Though receiving help from the Germans in running the café went very much against the grain, I had to accept it, if I did not wish to see the place reduced to a shambles. I am sure many of the local people among my customers agreed.

I believe that no worse calamity can befall a catering establishment than to be told one day: " Sorry! No more potatoes! " When the Germans came, stocks of potatoes in the island were not plentiful. Now the stocks were exhausted as far as catering establishments were concerned. Occasionally we were approached furtively with offers, but the prices demanded would have meant charging a king's ransom for them in the café, so we said: "No, thank you." Now and again we were able to pick up a few pig potatoes at a reasonable price, and as we still had linseed oil we could fry them. During the first year of the Occupation chips became a delicacy.

The first summer I bought a crop of raspberries as they stood, the price being such that I would have to have them picked. To derive as much profit from them as I could, I did the picking myself, rising with the lark to do so, or rather, as soon as the curfew allowed me. I collected Spot on the way.

Each morning I picked sufficient to provide fruit-and-cream teas. The "cream," I regret to say, was misnamed. It was, in fact, a concoction of ice-cream powder, powdered milk, soya bean flour and water. When taken from the refrigerator, where it had spent the night, it resembled dirty blocks of ice. But after a short time it would melt sufficiently to allow it to be poured over the fruit. It was often received with caustic remarks, but it was only after I had been accused on several occasions of serving frozen razor-blades, and I began to fear someone might actually cut his throat and sue me, that I decided to withdraw yet another item from the menu. I replaced it with a kind of milk pap, made from powdered milk. At least my clients could not harm themselves with that, and it was very filling.

Sometimes, when the local fishermen were allowed to go out a short distance in their boats, we were able to add variety to our fare with skate and mackerel. This was eaten with relish, by regulars only, accompanied by the stand-by swede to assure a balanced and not-too-rich diet. We had a very small bread ration which we dared not mention, and a margarine ration over which we had to stand guard. We also served a dish which we called "oat-cakes," though its basic ingredient was soya bean flour.

One dish, however, was a "constant." Even if we had to go without anything special on the other five days, the Saturday midday roast for "locals only" just had to appear. I managed not to miss a single Saturday roast right up to the time I embarked upon my compulsory travels, but great powers of persuasion were sometimes needed to convince the butcher that my reputation and indeed my custom were dependent on the joint he could let me have. On the very rare occasions on which he was quite unable to help I had to dip into my barrel of salted pork and overcome the emergency that way.

Before the War we had always scorned the limpet. But when it had been tested for edibility and was found to be not too bad, for the price of a free meal in the café I was always able to count on a 12-lb. basket, best supplier being Salah Ben Hadje, who seemed to be possessed of green fingers and secured the most succulent specimens. Removing the fish from the shells was a tedious task, and all hands would have to turn to. The meat would then be battered into some degree of flexibility and passed through the mincer. These processes completed, the result could be fashioned into a sort of fish-cake, a parsnip base being used to provide a somewhat unique flavour.

The limpet has one great draw-back, which we discovered only after one or two customers had nearly choked to death while eating it. The fibre by which it is attached to the shell is apparently averse to passing through the human gullet, and it is necessary to remove this indigestible part before serving.

To wash down the exotic dishes we produced, we could offer a delightful drink made from common acorns, euphemistically called coffee. For those preferring a beverage of less mud-like quality, we brewed a tea made from the common bramble which abounds in our hedgerows. Real tea was served as a surprise only on special occasions, well laced with bi-carb.

It was generally agreed by my regulars that the most tasty dish I set before them was the horse-meat with which, one Saturday, I was able to replace the roast. There were many requests for a repeat of this dish but though I kept my ear constantly to the ground for any rumour of a horse being shot or falling into a quarry, I had no success.

We once thought we had secured a special delicacy when a cormorant or duck diver came our way. When dressed, it very much resembled any table bird of similar size, but to the taste it was merely solidified salt, and when even the faithful Spot turned it down, it had to be cremated.

As I have indicated, Saturday lunch was our high spot,

and I always made a point of greeting personally each of my local customers at that meal. One Saturday, as I was making the rounds of the tables, one customer who was sitting by a window drew my attention to three aircraft approaching from the north, flying low over the sea, and coming straight for the harbour. We wondered why they were flying so low, but a second or two later we knew the reason. When immediately above the harbour they released their bombs, soared steeply over Castle Cornet and were on the way home before the explosions made The Home from Home rattle to its very bones. Though so brief, the raid was every effective. Admittedly, most unfortunately one or two friendly nationals lost their lives, but two direct hits were scored on German shipping in the harbour. Most valuable of all was the boost given to our morale. At least we could not complain of being forgotten.

This was not the only air-raid witnessed from the windows of The Home from Home. On several occasions soon after the evacuation of our families we had seen German reconnaissance planes flying over us at a great height. On the afternoon of Thursday, June 27th, 1940, it seemed that the enemy were satisfied that it would be safe for them to get a closer view of us, for an aircraft swooped in low from the east, almost skimming the waters of the harbour. Many of us in the café rushed to the windows when we heard the roar and were just in time to see the German markings on the underside of the wings as the pilot banked steeply over the town.

The appearance of this aircraft gave rise to much speculation, but we were not to be long in doubt. At tea-time the following day the café was crowded, and we were extremely fortunate in having no casualties when the German planes swooped down on the harbour with bombs and chattering machine guns which blew in all our windows and sprayed the stairway with bullets.

As if by magic people dived under the tables for shelter. A quick check showed that apart from cuts by flying glass there were no casualties, but possibly a further wave of bombers was on the way so quick action was needed. There was certainly no panic, but the great doubt about what would happen unnerved several. However, it was decided that the two best places for cover were in the cellar and under the staircase, so in very quick time I was able to transfer everyone from upstairs to a safer refuge.

When this operation was nearly completed Air Raid Warden Joe Eveson came in to tell me that Herbie Cambridge and P.C. "Chipper" Bougourd had been killed, among many others; he was of the opinion that there was more to come but not for a few minutes, so I took a look outside and was appalled to see the smoke and flames on the White Rock.

Returning to The Home from Home I found the cellar full. The women seemed to accept the situation better than the men. I recall that under the staircase two ladies from Sark were extremely concerned about their return to that island.

Fortunately, the "all clear" was sounded after what seemed an endless wait, and the work of clearing up and making secure started. As most of the staff lived in town and the possibility of further raids had to be considered I decided to transport all those who wished into the country. That night we squatted at Vazon Tea Rooms of which I had the key.

While there we learned that Guernsey had been declared an "open town," so we knew that no further raids were likely but that we were now in the hands of the enemy.

The entertainment which The Home from Home provided could be separated into two distinct categories: public for profit, private for pleasure. For the first, I encouraged people to stay with us as long as they liked, because while they remained, even after a meal, they would go on drinking acorn coffee or bramble tea, or take other supplementary fare, which all added first to my financial mill — and it needed it — for the margin of profit was not excessive.

The private entertainment would take place after the café was closed. It was by invitation only and was strictly non-profit making. With our families gone, there was nothing to attract us to our homes, and I felt I was doing something of a good turn by providing a place where my friends and closer acquaintances could pass the time in one another's company, for the pubs and bars were cheerless places in these days.

Once a week I used to organise a small dance, a trio providing the music. As the café was situated on the waterfront and people were always passing, naturally the strains of the music attracted a good many. Had I left the door open we should have been invaded by practically the whole island, so it was necessary for me to lock the door and stand guard over it.

As far as the islanders were concerned, there was little trouble. So long as they had a clean bill of health in the matter of collaboration with the enemy, and I knew they were lonely, they were welcome. Often, however, I would have trouble with the Germans, for as soon as the music started, they would begin banging on the door. If I let them bang without answering the majority would probably go away after a few moments. But there were a few persistent ones to whom it was necessary to open up. I could generally cope with an individual or even two, either by a polite refusal or a long story in English which they did not understand. But there were times when they would push me aside and stampede up the stairs. When this happened, the Alan Walters trio would pack up its instruments and go home. It is a matter for pride with me that no German ever took part in one of these private sessions.

Christmas 1941 found The Home from Home still plodding steadily along, serving its delicious acorn coffee and scrumptious limpet fish-cakes. The Germans were still honouring the ban on alcohol, and life passed in a kind of quiet half-truce, out of which we would occasionally be brought by the arrival of precious Red Cross messages from our loved ones in England. By this time, the messages were arriving with more regularity, about once every three months, though sometimes there were several at one delivery, and our return messages were also being received. I, for one, do not know how I should have survived without this contact with my family, slight though it was, and I am sure I was one among thousands who felt similarly.

Christmas, however, took on quite a different aspect for us now. We had nothing but memories, whereas for the children it meant practically nothing at all. To the island as a whole it marked yet another milestone in our strangely isolated existence. The Churches were filled by those who felt the season could be better appreciated in the sanctity of the House of Prayer. The Essential Commodities Committee did their best to mark the festival by issuing a little

46

extra of this and that — to do so they had had to conserve stocks for several weeks previously — but what was a joint of two ounces per person, including bone and gristle, as an encouragement to celebrate?

The Germans, on the other hand, still believed they were batting on a firm wicket. By now they had almost skinned most of the occupied countries and although the occupied were suffering acute privations, the occupiers had not yet remotely begun to feel the pinch. They were, therefore, determined to make a good splash.

For the occasion the Führer had, from the occupiers viewpoint, graciously sent to every member of his land, sea and air forces an autographed photograph of himself blowing out the candles on a Christmas tree — at least, I supposed that was what he was doing. The commissariat (provision depôt) had also sent up extra rations.

We knew this and we did not envy them. Let them have their celebrations, because very soon they would have nothing to celebrate. If we did not envy them, we believed they might have the decency not to flaunt their happiness under our noses; but that is exactly what they did to me.

One morning shortly before Christmas, while I was cleaning and cutting up swedes in the cellar, I received a visit from a German officer. He dallied only long enough to tell me that The Home from Home would be required by the German army for the festival, and to listen to my loud protests that the café had already been booked for some weeks. He appeared satisfied with this explanation and went away, but presently returned and summoned me from the cellar. " Who had booked the café? " he demanded, and I had to say a private party of islanders. It appeared that he had misunderstood me and had thought I had referred to another German unit. " In that case," he said, " you will cancel the booking and we shall hold our party here."

There was nothing else I could do but I had many misgivings. There was my precious stock, for example, particularly the linseed oil. Supposing that was raided! I should be sunk. Besides the Esse cooker, which was a temporary installation, was temperamental, and it was fatal to let it go out. To re-light it was a truly major operation.

I pointed this latter out and suggested I should stay in the kitchen to keep an eye on it — and on my stock. He found this a suitable suggestion and gave me the necessary permission and I was slightly relieved. At least I would be able to guard the acorn coffee and linseed oil with my life, if need be.

On the afternoon of the party a squad of German soldiers arrived to decorate the café, and I must admit they made a really good job of it. The ensemble was tastefully completed with greenery and holly and lit by candles in small lanterns.

When they had finished they stood guard over their stock, clearly awaiting the arrival of their master of ceremonies, and the customers who had remained, and my staff, looked on with interest and some amusement.

Presently the " big shot " arrived, and called for the " chief " who, I understood, was me. After giving me a very smart performance of " the old one-two sign with trimmings " he waved his arms in a wide gesture, shouting: " Aus! Alles aus! " and my customers and staff did his bidding with a few carefully chosen epithets inaudibly muttered, and left me with my unwanted guests.

It quickly became apparent that the big shot modelled himself closely on his dear Führer. He was soon throwing his weight about, demanding to know why I had not acquired more chairs. I decided then and there that the only term which could describe him fully would be a thoroughly nasty piece of work.

Early evening saw the first arrivals, preceded by a further fatigue party and two cooks. The former did a smart about-turn and went for more tables and chairs, and upon their return the seating plan was laid out. When all the preliminaries were completed to the satisfaction of the objectionable one, he left us with a round of Nazi salutes. From then on the café began to fill rapidly and I was ordered to go to the kitchen and stay there. Throughout the evening, and ever since, I dearly wished the R.A.F. could have been told that at least 200 N.C.O.s of the Wehrmacht were congregated under my roof.

When all were assembled, the food was brought in from outside and cauldrons of rum punch were set up in the kitchen. At the height of the proceedings, my curiosity got the better of me and, like a schoolboy, I asked for permission to leave the room. Before this could be granted, the authority of the objectionable one had to be obtained and he allowed me to go — under escort. I suppose he was wise. If I had thought of it in time and had had the courage, I might have been able to concoct a time-bomb and place it somewhere, where it would explode with effect.

I must be fair and say that what I saw on my brief journey to the lavatory made me wish that I could share it with guests of my own choosing. There was a Christmas air about the room, the lighting was discreet and the tables looked really attractive.

The rum punch soon began to make its influence felt, and soon music and song were coming from the café. I found myself wondering whether they had arranged to "bring on the dancing girls."

Presently, however, my thoughts began to wander to my family. What were they doing and thinking? Would next Christmas be a better one than the last two had been? Should we all be together again?

I was brought out of my reverie by the cook in charge of the rum punch taking compassion on me and offering me a ration. Thereafter he continued to press glasses of this excellent beverage on me and as time passed I seemed better able to understand their language and was even airing my own limited German vocabulary.

Even the objectionable one mellowed by the end of the evening. He came into the kitchen and beckoned me into the café, where he pointed out that nothing had been damaged. So that I might be able to open next morning, I pointed to this and that and understood that he agreed with all my suggestions. Presently he bade me "Good-night" with a final but rather sombre Nazi salute this time, and I wished he would fall downstairs and break his neck.

When I returned to the kitchen the cooks had already begun to clear up but they had decided that the remains of the punch must first be consumed. We had now reached the point of showing each other our family photographs. One of them, who came from Heidelberg, seemed a decent enough fellow and I promised to go and have a meal in his restaurant after the War. So far did I gain their confidence that they said they would leave the remainder of the stock in my charge until the morning.

As it was long after curfew, they offered to see me home. But though I appreciated their offer, I thought of the tarnish on my reputation were I to be seen arriving home accompanied by two Germans, so I decided to spend the remainder of the night in the café. After a combined rendering of " *Silent Night*," to show there were no ill feelings on either side, they departed.

It was my intention to open up early to give some of my friends a special Christmas breakfast, so I opened the blackouts and windows to freshen up the air, and settled down to rest in an easy chair by the Esse cooker. When I woke up I felt as if I had been hit all over with a cork hammer, but there was work to be done, and not much time.

Before I started moving and rearranging the tables, however, I went over the German stock to see if there was anything which would not be missed. Unfortunately, everything bore a heavy Wehrmacht stamp and I considered it would be too risky. One or two full bottles of rum had been opened, however, and I thought that if I took a little from each and filled up with water, they would taste much better. At the conclusion of my dispensing I had two medicine bottles of excellent rum.

When I had concealed my " perks " I separated the tables which did not belong to me and then swept the floor and picked up the odds and ends, which included a number of Adolf's photographs in varying states. Having picked out a clean one as a souvenir, I consigned the rest to the dustbin.

By dint of hard work I was ready by 9.30 a.m. As no staff were on duty by reason of the holiday, I let my two first regulars in myself and was in the middle of recounting the events of the previous night when we were disturbed by thunderous knocking on the front door.

When I opened it in burst the objectionable one, quite clearly in a murderously liverish mood. Where were all the decorations, tables and chairs? I showed him. Where was the stock? I took him to the kitchen. While he uncorked each open bottle of rum and sniffed it, I held my breath. But his judgment must have been impaired from the previous night's soaking for he passed them all and I heaved a sigh of relief — too soon!

The next moment he spied Adolf's pictures in the rubbish bin and then blew his top. Accusing me of everything from robbery to sabotage and, frankly, scaring the wits out of me, he made me pick the pictures from the bin and straighten them out and hand them over.

The fatigue party then arrived to remove their tables and chairs, and it was small consolation to note that he treated them to the same show of ferocious authority. Altogether I think he must have had a very enjoyable morning!

When the last chair and bottle had been carried away he stamped, quite forgetting to salute me, to the top of the stairs. Then he turned and gave me the " old one-two " — but without the trimmings.

When I rejoined my customers their first remark was how white I looked. Was I feeling ill? I did not bother to explain — they could not have failed to overhear all that had happened.

In due course I was paid in full for the use of the room.

Chapter IV

AGENT PROVOCATEUR

As we moved into the second year of the German Occupation stocks in most of the shops were almost non-existent. Traders opened only a few hours a day, and apart from the weekly rations supplied by the Essential Commodities Committee and the very occasional extras secured by our Purchasing Commission in France, mostly wines, there was little or nothing to sell. Now the Black Market really began to come into its own.

My personal problem was pipe tobacco. In a desperate effort to find a supply I tried any reasonable substitute, including dried bramble leaves, for which I eventually acquired the taste—but only after great perseverance—and dried rose petals. One unfortunate quality of bramble-leaf tobacco is that while you were smoking it, it gave off a continuous shower of sparks, and if there was a wind, these sparks presented a very real danger of setting light to your clothing.

At this time I was living with friends and as my hostess was very house-proud, I usually took the precaution of emptying my pipe before entering the house. On one occasion, however, I did not do this and as bad luck would have it, I had scarcely entered the drawing-room with my pipe still in my mouth when I sneezed. Not only did it take me what seemed an age to dowse every spark which settled on the settee, carpet and other furnishings, but I almost had to call in the Fire Brigade to help me.

All this led to a rather unpleasant incident.

To get hold of a stock of French or German cigarettes and tobacco, I explored every possible channel and took advantage of any opportunity to do a deal. In this, I was only one of many and competition was fierce.

One day a friend of mine offered me a large quantity of German cigarettes "no questions asked". The price was right and as my friend was in a responsible position, I felt sure that the source of supply was fairly safe. The bargain was struck, the cigarettes delivered and stowed away. Later I exchanged some of them for pipe tobacco and, as the remainder did not interest me personally, I resold some to my friends.

I was in the café one afternoon when a Guernseyman, whom I knew only by sight, came in. He had heard, he said, that I had cigarettes for sale. He was a non-smoker himself but could he possibly have a couple of packets for a foreign worker who had rendered him good service?

I had doubts about this deal, but in the end sold him two packets and he went happily away. Not for one moment did I doubt his sincerity—my doubts centred on the wisdom of an islander giving a foreign worker a packet of German cigarettes—and I am quite sure he did not realise he was being duped.

Within the hour a foreign worker came into the café with a German Feldgendarme or policeman. I was about to have my tea at the back of the café but they picked me out at once and came over to me. Producing the cigarettes, because the German policeman apparently did not speak English, the worker demanded to know how many of these cigarettes I had and where I had obtained them.

Since I knew that the most superficial search would disclose the cigarettes, there was nothing for me to do but produce them and hand them over. But I did manage to bluff my way out of revealing the source of supply by saying that a foreign worker, whom I would not be able to identify again, had sold them to me. They then questioned my assistant who, fortunately and truthfully, knew nothing.

After a brief conference in German between the policeman and the so-called foreign worker, I and my assistant, Harry Ferguson, Jnr., were ordered to accompany them to police headquarters. In an effort to make light of our situation to the rest of my worried staff, I called out to them to keep my tea hot as I would be back for it soon. To my great surprise, the policeman called out in good English: "That's what he thinks!" and my spirits sank considerably.

At police headquarters in Queen's Road we were not separated but kept for several hours under close supervision. Late in the evening we were interrogated singly and then told to sign long statements in English, which we did.

All hope of being released that night was dashed when we were informed that we should be kept in custody until our statements had been checked. I hoped their time would not be too much taken up with other matters for them to do the checking quickly as I had no desire to spend much time in prison.

It surprised me how easily one could be introduced into a German prison. There were no formalities of any kind such as one might have expected from so orderly a people as the Germans. Everything was apparently highly organised.

We could not have chosen a worse time to be locked up, for the prison was crammed with recalcitrant Guernsey policemen and as all the cells were full, they started doubling up. My cell was one on the outside on the first floor where I was provided with a sack of straw for a mattress and two blankets.

My cell-mate, one of the policemen, told me I was lucky not to have been arrested before. The Home from Home had, on several occasions, been the cause of concern to the local police who, aware that Germans were barred from our private sessions, feared an incident between my clients and the Germans, in which they did not wish to become involved. In fact, on one occasion when I requested assistance, I was told to sort it out myself.

In our restricted space we talked far into the night until a warder on his rounds heard us and treated us to some of the choicest German, which I have always regretted I could not understand.

There was a gap under the door almost wide enough to crawl through. It admitted a draught that seemed to us to have the qualities of an Arctic gale. We thought that we might exclude this icy blast if one of us pushed his mattress right up to the door and slept there. I suggested that as my companion was the younger man, he would undoubtedly prefer to perform this service, but he argued that my stay was likely to be shorter than his and suggested we should draw lots. The first time I won; the second time he won—and the third. So I pushed my mattress up to the gap.

Next morning I was as stiff as a board and as cold as charity. Prison breakfasts notoriously lack imagination, but the one served to me was so abnormal in quality, that only the fact that I had had nothing to eat since the previous day's lunch stopped me from refusing it with my compliments.

In the middle of the morning the German police came for me and took me to their headquarters. During the afternoon I was entertained to a kind of double-act identity parade. First, I was introduced to a selection of shady looking individuals and told to pick out the one who had sold me the cigarettes. Naturally I could not do that but I made a show of examining each one closely before saying no. Then the positions were reversed and I was taken into another room where three men were asked if they had ever sold any goods to me. Fortunately, they denied ever having seen me before.

Back in the waiting room I was joined by my assistant, who had been put through the same processes and after a time we were driven back to the gaol for another cold and miserable night.

The second morning I was left alone in the cell, while my companion was taken for interrogation. He returned shortly before the midday food was served and I gathered he and his associates had had a very sticky time. One of their number had tried to ingratiate himself with the Germans, apparently, by trying to implicate his friends in charges which, if they had stuck together, could have been brushed aside. As a result, for the rest of the day the prison resounded with threats and abuse shouted from cell to cell. By evening the noise had become so great that the German guards threatened to shoot the next man who made a sound.

I huddled down in a corner of my cell to keep well out of this conflict. It upset me more than I can say to hear my own countrymen behaving in this way, so my reactions can be imagined when, a short time after the turmoil had subsided, the German policeman came into my cell and said: " Mr. Stroobant, you are free! You may go home! "

At this time I was closely connected with the amateur theatricals and as a musical comedy was due to be performed that evening, I went straight to the theatre. A particular friend of mine, Stanley Smith, was holding the stage as I went in and although he had a shocking voice, at that moment I was convinced I had never heard sweeter sounds issuing from any human throat.

No doubt my sudden appearance caused a slight stir, which made the singer glance in my direction. What he saw completely threw him off his stroke and he lost touch with the orchestra. By the time he had finished his number the musicians were almost ready to go home.

After the show I received many congratulations at regaining my freedom and at my lodgings I was greeted like a long lost brother, despite the fact that during my absence the Germans had not only made a thorough search of my room, but of the whole house. Next morning at the café the congratulations began again, but a remark of one of my customers made me cut them short. While I had been away, he said, the quality of the tea had greatly improved.

Alarmed I dashed to the tea stock and discovered that not only had the daily ration been greatly exceeded, but that no bicarbonate of soda had been used. By a slight increase in the proportions of the latter and a reduction in the quantity of the former, I was soon able to make up the loss, but not, I regret to say, without having to face the accusation of several of my clients that I was serving bath-water.

The majority of my friends and acquaintances had never expected to see me again so for a time I was a natural centre of attraction. Many conflicting stories had been put into circulation concerning me. Regretfully I must admit that the reports of my connection with espionage, sabotage or an underground organisation had no basis in fact, and that nothing honourable in support of our country's war effort had led to my arrest.

CHAPTER V

DEPORTATION

T HE PROBLEM OF SUPPLIES grew increasingly acute, and
The Home from Home existed on practically a day-to-day
basis. But the worse things became, the greater service I
believed myself to be doing for my friends and customers. I
was quite prepared to continue the struggle until there was
not one scrap of food for caterers to be obtained in the island,
and would have gone on doing so had I not been personally
affected by a German order promulgated in the late summer
of 1942.

For some time it had been rumoured that all men of
military age were to be removed from the island and stories
varied from forced labour camps on the Continent, internment camps on the Continent or internment in the island.
We did not baulk at the logic of such a move, for we recognised that we in this group could become a distinct nuisance
to the Germans in the event of an Allied landing, but when
we considered the strength of the fortifications and of the
German garrison, which numbered about 30,000, we considered an Allied landing not very likely and, therefore, ourselves safe.

However, our hopes were soon to be shattered and when
the order came its contents provided a considerable shock.

All people of British birth—this included me because,
though my father was a Guernseyman, I had been born in
England—were to register at the Feldkommandantur. The
order affected not just men of military age, whether Guernseymen or English-born Islanders, but men of British birth
of all ages—and women and children too! All were to be
interned in Germany. It was the wrenching of elderly and
often infirm men and women from their homes, and the
removal of the children which we could not understand,
as it seemed that the Germans were inviting a liability and
the only solution we could think of was that it was a reprisal

for some act by the Allies somewhere involving the internment of German civilians.

When the complete list of those to be deported was
eventually issued the distress caused was tragic. A few of
the older people, not knowing what the Fates might have
in store for them, took their own lives. The younger ones,
for the most part, accepted the situation philosophically, even
when it began to emerge that some of their own age-group
had somehow managed to escape the axe. Good luck to them
if they could wangle it! No hard feelings!

The official German notice reached all those selected for
deportation, myself included, on 18th September, 1942. They
were to report in two parties at the Gaumont Cinema, the
first at noon on Monday, 21st September, the second on
Wednesday, 23rd September.

As soon as those to be deported found out who were to
be their companions in distress, we all got together and
decided to have a grand finale to our stay in Occupation
Guernsey; and what more suitable place could be found for
such a celebration than The Home from Home? The most
important people to contact now were those who could
provide some form of liquid refreshment, and any gift was
matched with an invitation to attend our " do ". Our scouts
went out with a set plan of campaign, and the degree of their
success was measured by the ever-increasing stocks which
they brought in.

The farewell was taking place in mid-September and the
curfew was at 10 o'clock. But I think that nearly everyone
was prepared to ignore it for once, even the Germans, who
were not happy about the women and children being included
in the order, and seemed to be prepared to turn a blind eye
to several of our activities.

Once again it is really surprising what can be unearthed
in an emergency. There was certainly no function since pre-
war days that could compare with our party in the matter
of food and drink. We did not trouble about the service as
everything was on the donors of the liquid feast. The
deportees had the privilege of inviting their friends, and the
result was a capacity house.

As I was expecting trouble I had taken the precaution
of having a short speech written for me in German advising
all German nationals who might come along and demand

admission, that this was a final party for the people who were being taken to Germany and we would appreciate being left alone. Armed with this I hoped for the best.

We started on the dot and the trio really went to town. For the occasion we had augmented the band by the addition of a top-class bass player, Hank Reeve, who was really a wonderful acquisition. As the evening progressed so the tempo increased, and a crowd gathered outside. Much of my time was taken up with having regretfully to refuse admission to regular supporters and friends, but the place was packed and the floor was not taking the strain too well. An inspection proved alarming; we were advised to keep near the walls. In addition to this, I was also employed in making frequent readings of my "not welcome" address. The band had instructions not to waste a single moment but to press on regardless; and if any Jerry forced his way in, it was up to the crowd to make him feel unwanted. The odd one or two did beat me to it while I was reading my announcement but when they reached the top of the stairs they were so heavily outnumbered that they did not stay.

When the time came finally to break up the proceedings, the deportees were asked to assemble in the middle of the room. After a few informal but nonetheless sincere words had been spoken from both sides—those who were and those who were not going—everyone joined in the singing of *Auld Lang Syne* and I think that I have never heard it sung with greater emotion than I heard it then. Something would still have been lacking, however, had we finished this night of parting on that note, so I put out the lights, took down the black-outs and opened wide all the windows.

The band knew what was expected of them and I am sure that everyone within hearing of The Home from Home must always remember the singing of *The White Cliffs of Dover*, *Land of Hope and Glory*, *There'll Always be an England* and *Auld Lang Syne* by nearly two hundred of their countrymen on the verge of deportation.

After *Rule Britannia* came the climax, the only fitting climax to such an occasion—the singing of *God Save the King*, which we were assured next morning by the police on duty at the Town Church, could be clearly heard by them.

The Germans made no attempt to interfere in any way. We had all been prepared to take any reasonable chance at any time, but as nothing seemed to matter now to so many of us we took risks that night which formerly we would have thought twice about. There was many a tear shed at the parting. Perhaps we were a little bit moved by alcohol, but I am certain that the majority of the tears were genuine and that the moment of farewell is still clear in the memories of many of us who were present.

Although we unattached men spent our last night in this way, there were very many who were unable to treat the approaching day with such a light heart. We knew that several tragic partings were taking place. Families were being split up and many were saying farewell to parents and grand-parents in the knowledge that it must be the final farewell. There were men and women who were frightened of what lay ahead of them in a strange enemy country and neither could console the other. There were children who had done no harm in their lives, except to be born to a father who himself had been born on English soil. There were tearful partings with faithful pets. Children could not understand what was going on for their minds were incapable of taking in the hate and cruelty of war.

In the knowledge of these tragic partings, it was with a certain feeling of relief that I thought of my own loved ones now safe in the Motherland, where they would be spared much pain and grief. But I had one parting to make myself which I found very difficult. It was with my faithful four-legged friend Spot, who, even on that eventful night, had stayed in the kitchen out of harm's way, but near at hand in case his presence should be required. I cannot prove that there is an understanding between man and beast which could convey to him my thoughts, but I seemed to sense that he knew how sad I felt, and how much his company had meant to me during the strange days of the Occupation.

It had become obvious to those in official positions, that some provisions would have to be supplied for the deportees, who, when they were moved from the assembly point at the Gaumont Cinema in St. Julian's Avenue, might be kept in the prohibited area of the harbour for goodness knows how long before they eventually embarked. The decision had been taken, therefore, to supply them with a meal before they left and a package containing sandwiches, fruit and tobacco or cigarettes for the journey.

As a result of the very raw deal I had received after my previous efforts at the kiosk during the evacuation operation, I had made up my mind that giving service to the public in time of an emergency was a risk I would not take again. So when I was approached by an official, Vernon Le Maitre, with a request to undertake the necessary catering, I shied. However, when I had thought it over I felt differently and as I was due to go with the first party and the meal might be the last decent one we should have for many a long day, I consented determined that we should feed off the finest food available. I was then promptly transferred to the second party.

When I agreed, I was told that the States of Guernsey would provide meat, potatoes, vegetables, milk and bread in good quantities. This generosity prompted me to make a gesture of my own. Among my most treasured possessions were several large tins of ham which I had stored away with great secrecy in a safe place, intending to keep them for Liberation celebrations if hunger had not got the better of me by then. But this, though no celebration, was an occasion almost equal to Liberation! So I brought them out and handed them to the sandwich makers, who spent hours cutting them into wafer-thin slices.

Besides this, I thought I would try to supplement the States donation with a hard-boiled egg. If I could find enough eggs to give one to each man, woman and child, I knew what a great treat they would be. Though eggs had long since disappeared from our tables, I nevertheless believed there might be some about somewhere and rather than go into the nooks and crannies of the Black Market, I put an advertisement in the newspapers.

"WANTED: 1,000 eggs immediately, 8s. per doz. offered."

The response to my appeal was instantaneous and breath-taking. Very few asked the price I had offered, which was above the controlled price (only when I returned to the Island after the Liberation did I become aware that I had infringed the price-control Orders and made myself liable once more to court action—though this time I was not arraigned) and would either accept only the controlled or a lower price, while the others insisted on making a gift of their eggs, regretting they had not more.

With the problem of the packed food thus solved, my major headache was how to cook a substantial meal for four hundred and fifty or so people on the assembly point and at the same time to do justice to the excellent raw material supplied by the States of Guernsey Control of Essential Commodities Committee. The actual dining-room, which was used for feeding the forced labourers working in the harbour area, was fine; but forced labourers were not provided with hot or extensive meals and there was no kitchen! So, after seeking advice and contacting likely sources, we secured the loan of a large copper boiler. The idea was to suspend this from a tripod over a fire in a brazier—if we could get a brazier—and as a method of cooking it did not appeal to me at all, so I went on searching.

Local officials, led by Louis Guillemette, eventually provided the solution. Obviously they did not want to see their meat ruined, so they asked the Germans for the use of a field kitchen, which the Germans provided. Here should be mentioned the great help given by Mme. Pommier, of Fountain Street. If it was possible for the Germans to feel ashamed, I am quite certain that all the Germans on the scene that day must have been pricked in their consciences by the sight of old men and women, delicate youngsters and tiny children being torn from their homes and all that was dear to them, bewildered and helpless, and apprehensive of what their fate in the Third Reich would be.

In the Sarnian Fruit Company's large store in the Pollet, conveniently near the assembly point, a small army of willing workers spent long hours cleaning vegetables and peeling potatoes. Several of them whose belts were already drawn in a number of notches, must have felt very envious of the meal they were preparing. Such food in such quantities had not been seen for a long time.

The Germans also provided cooks with the field kitchen and these men helped us all they could. When it became apparent that one kitchen would be inadequate, a second was called for and quickly arrived on the scene, and soon the lamb stew was sending off a pleasing aroma.

Now that we had everything we wanted, including plates and cutlery from various sources, we preferred to paddle our own canoe without appealing for assistance. The Germans supervising the deportations seemed to appreciate this and merely stood looking on without interfering, though one or two truculent members tried to be difficult, notably the German harbour-master. When at last the meal was ready, everyone agreed that the States of Guernsey had given them a wonderful send-off. Not only was the food appetising, but the order of the day was that all were to eat as much as they could hold, if the food lasted for this to be possible—and it did.

During a lull in the operations, I took the opportunity of inspecting the shipping provided by the Germans, and was appalled to find two old tramp vessels which had obviously been used for carrying coal. Both were in a filthy condition and were in ballast. With weather conditions bad —the wind was blowing with almost gale force—even for experienced sailors it would have been suicidal to put to sea in them. The accommodation for the passengers had been arranged in the deep holds, where the only seating was a few long forms which would have been thrown about by the movement of the ship, even in calm weather. In fact the transport was so unbelievably primitive that I was sure many of the deportees could not possibly survive the journey.

I protested to any German within hearing, but was met with only disinterested shrugs of the shoulders. We had been told that embarkation was to begin shortly and though I think some of the Germans were alarmed by the idea of sending the ships to sea in a storm, sure enough the by-now alarmed deportees—many of whom were leaving the island for the first time since they had arrived on it—were soon being herded aboard. Even the most able-bodied had difficulty in climbing down the steep ladders, while for the old and infirm it was practically impossible. The darkness of the holds frightened the children, who began to cry and to these sad sounds was added the disquieting noise of the water lapping against the sides of the holds.

To their undying credit, the States' officials protested vehemently to the Germans, and it gave me great pleasure to add my vocal support. But only a decision by the highest German authority could vary the orders, so a deputation was immediately sent to him.

I was honoured by being included in this deputation and, on our side, words were not minced. After much evasion and cross-talk by the Germans, it was, however, decided to hold up the sailings until the weather had abated.

Though the decision was received with great rejoicings by those on board, their actual physical plight was only slightly eased by it, for they were not permitted to disembark. By now the holds were reminiscent of the Black Hole of Calcutta, chiefly on account of the sanitation facilities which were of the most barbaric type. We tried to make life a little more bearable for them by securing extra blankets but after this we were ordered out of the harbour area by the Germans, and though we left our friends with many misgivings, we knew that for the night, at least, they would be safe.

The decision to delay the sailing also produced another problem for us. We were particularly anxious that the deportees should not have to break into their food packages before they got on their way, for no one could say how long the journey to their final destination would take.

So I at once went into a huddle with my helpers and decided that we must make more sandwiches and provide hot coffee when the curfew was lifted at 6 o'clock the next morning. It was a simple matter to find volunteers but as the curfew was strict we thought it would be unwise to ask permission for too many to stay with us, though it would mean no sleep or rest throughout the night for those who did stay. Our task was made lighter, however, by the generous offer from Mr. Mentha, manager of a leading hotel, of the use of their kitchen, and when a quick delivery of the necessary bread and sandwich fillings was made, we set to.

During the night someone suddenly asked what we were going to give the babies and young children, since acorn coffee would not be suitable for them. It was thought that some sort of milk diet ought to be provided.

Fortunately, among the helpers was Doctor Sutcliffe, who knew where there were supplies of Lactine, if only we could get at it. At that time doctors were among the few classes of civilians holding all-night passes and who were permitted to use their cars in an emergency.

We declared an emergency and without hesitation the doctor offered to get his car, pick me up at the hotel and drive out into the country to search out George de Garis, manager of Le Riche's Store where the Lactine was. The

sticklers for the letter of the law—the Germans made no protest about my luggage [See plate 2].

We sailed at night, in much better ships than provided for the first party, escorted by a flak-ship to the French port of St. Malo. The recent storm had given way to calm, and our journey was not too unpleasant. From St. Malo we went by rail to Dorsten in the Ruhr, where we joined up with the first party and with some of those deported from Jersey.

I have always considered myself lucky to have been in the second party, after we had been reunited with our friends of the first party and learned what they had suffered. The sea had still been choppy when they left St. Peter Port and their unsuitable ships did not take kindly to it. Mothers and babies suffered particularly.

It rained during most of the five hours of the journey to St. Malo and on arrival there they had been held up while their ship passed through the locks into the harbour. The good people of St. Malo, though accustomed to German methods, were alarmed at seeing pregnant women and young babies in the party and attempted to show their sympathy in tangible form by offering gifts of grapes, though the Germans soon put a stop to this. Then there had been long delays again before the train started.

They did, however, miss one incident which befell us in the second party. We were parked in a siding at Cologne, not far from the cathedral and over by the Hohenzollern bridge during an air-raid warning. It was night time and the darkness added to the alarm which we naturally felt for the women and children in the party.

The camp to which we were sent—it was deserted when the first party arrived—was in the heart of the thickly populated industrial Ruhr, not at all a good site for a civilian internment camp, we thought, since we were surrounded by many legitimate objectives for air attack. The surrounding countryside was low and flat, and the barrage of guardian balloons did not add to our peace of mind. Besides this, the camp was below the level of the canal, which ran almost parallel with one side of its perimeter, and the nearby great lock-gates, which had been disturbed by an air-raid two nights before, did not seem to us to augur well for our physical safety. However, we had to make the best of it, though it was a poor best, for by the time all the Channel Islands deportees arrived the camp was unbearably overcrowded.

To make matters worse, our accommodation was extremely primitive, consisting of a number of army huts heated by slow-combustion stoves. For the first time in my life I realised that there are people who do not require air to breathe, and the first night in the overcrowded hut was spent in a kind of warfare, as those of the fresh-air cult opened windows which were immediately shut by those of the "fug" cult. By morning, those sleeping in the upper tiers of the bunks resembled smoked herrings.

The most disturbing part of this first sample of internment was watching the small children approach the barbed wire. You could see in their faces their utter inability to understand why they should be reprimanded by a big man in jackboots whose words they could not understand but whose tone and manner frightened them.

One of our most serious problems was obtaining suitable diets for the children and for the rapidly mounting number of hospital cases. The hut set aside for the hospital was soon overfull and since the Germans supplied no nurses, those who had a little medical or first-aid knowledge among us, were required to do what they could for the relief of the sick.

Though there were a few who adopted an attitude of "couldn't care less," the majority turned to work with good will. Apart from a few scenes about Jack having more food than his neighbour, and a massed raid on the kitchen in an attempt to discover why there was sand in the cabbage, within a short time we attained a degree of law and order.

We had, of course, been somewhat conditioned to leisure by the Occupation at home and it was not long before an entertainment and sports meeting was held to decide on means to keep us occupied.

We were very fortunate in having a German Commandant who not only had blood in his veins and a humane nature, but had been a P.O.W. in England during the First World War. He remembered the considerate treatment he had received then, and clearly wished to repay some of the kindness. Out of his own pocket he bought milk for the children from nearby P.O.W. camps, and some of us were convinced that it was due to his efforts that Red Cross parcels speedily began to reach us. As he was a pork-butcher in civilian life, I am sure that those Guernsey and Jersey mothers who have reason to be grateful for his kindness to their children will hope that his pigs will always be lean ones!

The Channel Islands deportees stayed at Dorsten for seven weeks, but a week earlier the unattached men were singled out and sent to a camp in south-east Germany. Before setting off they were told to elect their own leader for the journey, and a canvass of candidates was made. While we had been at Dorsten I had seen the sort of existence led by the camp leader, Garfield Garland, so I have no one but myself to blame for allowing my name to go forward. There were only three candidates, and as the other two men did not get on very well—and this was realised by the rest—it was practically inevitable that the doubtful honour should fall to me.

I had not assumed my responsibilities long before I realised what I had let myself in for. The train journey to our new camp would take twelve hours, we were told, and we were issued with rations for this period. But even if the train had started on time, some of the party would have consumed the bulk of their provisions before it started. Whether they measure time in Germany on a different basis from us or whether there was any other reason for it, at all events at the end of twelve hours we were still in the Ruhr, and it did not take a complicated mathematical calculation to realise that the timetable had slipped.

At the end of twenty-four hours the belly-aches started; and so did mine, though it was of a different nature. What was I going to do about their food and drink supply?

Their guess as to what I might be able to do was as good as mine, but as the big chief of the outfit I thought I ought to attempt something. It was a long road I travelled going through the multitude of underlings until I reached the German officer in charge of us. This gentleman was not helped by the language difficulty, for I was certain that he said something about "coming up" and, accordingly, I advised my party that food was on the way.

Shortly afterwards we pulled into a siding and I sincerely believed that this meant food. I hoped so, for the men were by this time more restive than ever. However, several hours elapsed, the train was still in the siding and there was no sign of even a crust. As our stomachs were by now so empty that our navels were sticking to our back-bones, I decided that I must move once again, and once more climbed the Jacob's ladder of underlings until I reached the big chief —only to find that he had temporarily left the train.

When I returned to my compartment I found a deputation waiting on me, who let me know, quite frankly, what they thought of my leadership and what they would do if they had the job, and indicated that if I did not soon show a marked improvement my post would be declared vacant and a new man appointed.

After what seemed an eternity, the train pulled out, and I knew that I must make a face-saving effort. This time, however, I took the precaution of taking with me an interpreter who spoke German with a Welsh accent. Having been ushered into the Presence, through my mouthpiece I informed him that we had been given twelve hours' rations thirty-six hours before and that the men were rather hungry. As it was " fresh " in our carriages—in fact, it was perishing cold, but I was trying to be diplomatic—a nice hot drink would also be appreciated. After several " Jah, jah! " I gathered that we should definitely eat at the next stop. When would that be? He could not say precisely, but soon. And that was all the information I could take back with me. If I could bring myself to record the comments of my companions, little purpose would be served, for the words would burn the paper on which I write; but as by this time I was as fed up as they were and did not take kindly to being looked up on as a Simple Simon, stubbornly—and foolishly—I stood my ground.

Forty hours after we entrained at Dorsten, we ran into Rosenheim. Here, the German Red Cross provided us with a really man-sized meal and, fearing a repetition of what had already happened, everyone tucked away as much as he could.

The fact that they had now eaten and drunk gave the men a more roseate outlook and I was left alone to enjoy the magnificent scenery as we skirted the foothills of the Alps and came into Upper Bavaria. But I not only scanned the scenery, I made good use of the opportunity to study my companions. Although I had always considered myself a doubtful judge of character, I separated one or two who, I believed, would prove to be thorns in my side when we arrived eventually at our new home; and I was so startlingly right!

We came at last to Laufen in the middle of the night.

CHAPTER VI

LAUFEN

THE LITTLE BAVARIAN TOWN of Laufen is not particularly noteworthy, its outstanding feature being the Schloss Laufen, formerly the country residence of the Archbishop of Salzburg [See frontispiece]. It stands on a spur which forces the river Salzac into a hairpin bend. Like most other rivers having their sources in the Bavarian Alps, the Salzac is a river of extreme moods. In the spring the melting mountain snows turn it into a raging torrent which appears always to threaten the little town as it rushes madly around the acute bend, but as summer approaches it steadies down and in parts becomes navigable, while in the autumn it is reduced to a narrow stream of leisurely moving water.

The only bridge spanning the river just here is dominated by the Schloss and connects Laufen with the Austrian village of Obendorf. It was here that the beautiful carol "*Silent Night: Holy Night*" was composed. The people are countrymen and being Bavarian are a friendly folk. In normal times I imagine they made very agreeable companions. The surrounding district is undulating and purely agricultural.

Nature seems to play fantastic tricks in this lovely country. The winter snows vanish almost overnight and give way to green countryside in which, presently, crops appear to spring up even as one watches.

It was here, then, that we arrived in the middle of the night almost forty-eight hours after leaving Dorsten.

We were formed up outside the station to march to Schloss Laufen, which was to be our home for the next three years. We were all glad of the opportunity to stretch our legs and when the order to march was given we stepped out briskly to the accompaniment of a mouth-organ. Presently the mouth-organ was itself accompanied by weird noises which soon resolved themselves into songs. Had there been any spectators, they might legitimately have mistaken us for the remnants of Fred Karno's army.

In an effort to improve the general marching, whether I had the necessary authority or not, I went back down the ranks. My entreaties to keep in step had the desired effect and we got well into the swing, and by the time we arrived at the Schloss gates I was feeling proud to be marching at the head of this motley crew.

On arrival at the castle, we were paraded and instructed in military camp routine. From that moment, we were told, we would be subject to military discipline and we had better therefore watch our step. On being dismissed we were deloused and, this operation completed, were shown to our new quarters, having first been issued with cutlery and bedding.

The Schloss was already partly occupied by a contingent of deportees from Jersey. Although there has always been a superficial friendliness between Jerseymen and Guernseymen, the natural rivalry is such that the feelings have never, by any stretch of the imagination, amounted to affection. As it was, from this first middle of the night encounter until we finally disbanded I cannot recall a single instance in which insular feelings were the cause of discord.

As I was the leader of the larger contingent, the leader of the present occupants, Roy Skingle, offered to vacate his position so that I might become Camp Senior. When I failed to persuade him to accept that post—I must confess I did not try very hard—he agreed to act as my deputy. Between us and a council of advisers we apportioned out all camp offices and departments equally between Jerseymen and Guernseymen and tranquillity reigned. I am quite sure that the friendships made at Laufen, and the other Channel Islands camps during this period have helped considerably in the better post-war spirit which now exists between the islands.

There were also among us a number of Americans who lived in small rooms on the other side of the parade ground, each room holding about 20 men. Some of these internees were actually American civilians who had been trapped in enemy territory by the United States' sudden entry into the War on 7th December, 1941. The majority, however, claimed American citizenship through their fathers who, having emigrated to America, had since returned to their fatherland but had still kept up their American citizenship. In many cases these Americans could speak no English but only their mother tongue. Besides these there were a few who claimed citizenship of one or other of the Central American or South American States. So, altogether it was quite a mixed bag which made demands on my leadership, though the American section very soon had its own organization and leadership.

Anyone who has experienced life in an internment camp will appreciate that for their leaders the most difficult duty is the enforcement of discipline. In military prisoner of war camps you have the framework of discipline already set up by the system of ranks and, what is more, the principles of discipline which communal living necessitates, if it is to succeed at all, has been imbued in all members of the camp.

In a civilian internment camp, under German military command, on the other hand, you have a number of people who have never been used to collective discipline, who revolt at any attempt to enforce such discipline on the grounds that it strikes at that most jealously defended of all human rights, the liberty of the individual. Yet in a civilian internment camp there is as great a need for discipline as in any similar military institution. Without it any form of communal living must eventually deteriorate into a state of anarchy, for there is no doubt that discipline keeps in check the peculiarities of the individuals—and we all have our peculiarities, heaven knows — which is not noticeable in smaller circles and with absolute freedom of movement, but which become extremely noticeable when large numbers are herded together in close quarters from which there is no escape. The peculiarities then become the source of animosities and at last outright quarrels. A good example is the early friction between the fresh air cult and the "fug" cult over the matter of open or closed windows at night.

Consider the mixed bag we were. We included the ex-colonel who had shot tigers at a range of three feet and the simple fisherman from Sark who was entitled to and claimed equal rights with this gentleman — who could not (or who would not) understand that his rank and title meant nothing here. There was the super-executive type used to the attentions of a large staff, both at the office and at home, who was scarcely capable of blowing his own nose. There were the intellectual types who claimed that life was unbearable without their music and who almost wept on your shoulder when you suggested that they should learn to play a comb covered with tissue paper. There were the "leaning" types who were completely lost without a counter for support. There was the investor who lost weight not so much from the lack of food as from the constant nagging thought of the money he was losing every hour he was out of touch with the Stock Exchange. The student of religion found it very heavy going sharing a room with 40 men who all swore like troopers in most exotic terms. The perpetual moaner ought to have come into his own with so many legitimate grievances, but he overplayed his role by concocting imaginary ones.

I was often tempted to administer sharp kicks on their back-side, for I was sure it was the only efficacious treatment. There were the highly sexed who genuinely suffered from being cut off from normal relations; and all of us at some time or other felt the lack of female company.

Fortunately the large majority were normal, rational men, ordinary men, if you like, who took the situation in hand and really did everything they could to make life bearable for their companions and, incidentally, for themselves; they were the ones who accepted any fatigue with good grace and who made light of their hardships; though they had insufficient to eat, they would organise competitions to see which of them could cut most slices from his meagre ration of German bread. Often some of the resulting slices, if put up for sale would have fetched good prices as lampshades. These were the men who, by their example, helped me most, for it was discipline that was certainly my biggest headache when I took over the leadership of Laufen.

The camp office was at any time of the day or night subjected to without-warning visits from one or parties of irate internees protesting either a warranted or imaginary grievance which was impossible to solve.

As a measure of trying to short-circuit as much trouble as possible, every evening I, accompanied by a member of the office staff as escort, used to go on a tour of the whole camp, even to the American side, and in each barrack room I would ask: "Any complaints?"

We found it advantageous to start the journey in " Hell's Kitchen " or " Chinatown " — here the " fug " cult had an overwhelming majority and the official party scarcely had time to enter before shouts of " Shut the bloody door " issued from all corners.

It is on record that one night an inmate, who had slept through our visit, suddenly realised that air had seeped into the room. In his semi-conscious state he echoed his war-cry, but unfortunately for him his appeal fell on the unreceptive ears of the German guards who were taking the night tally, and having been hastily summoned from his nice warm nest he spent the night in the " cooler."

Each night our party, having decided that the only course for our mission to " Chinatown " was to leave the inmates to " stew in their own juice," we came up for air feeling braced to meet whatever might come.

The route followed diverse channels but always ended in Snob Alley at the " House of Lords." By the time this point was reached the party had gathered sufficient general knowledge of camp conditions in general and their own status in particular, to enable them to answer any question the " wise men of the east " could throw at them.

Unless you had come with me, I am quite sure that you would not credit the silly answers the enquiry " Any complaints? " brought forth. Mind you, I expected to get some outlandish requests or complaints, but it seemed to me that men whom you would ordinarily have thought to have been sensible fellows, became touched in the mind by even a few days' internment. Some demanded eggs for breakfast on Sundays — when practically all the eggs produced in the Third Reich went to the Russian front — and German civilians had almost forgotten what they looked like. Others were quite insistent that the Germans would provide film shows if I put in a request for them. Others demanded an increase in the bread ration, but I knew the chances of getting this were as hopeless as the eggs.

Many made no attempt to move from their beds when I went into the rooms, or take any apparent interest. I am convinced, however, that this nightly tour greatly helped in keeping the camp quiet, at least until the Red Cross food parcels began to arrive. If these parcels had failed, goodness knows what would have happened. I have a feeling that I should not have survived to pound this typewriter.

Since I was determined that everyone in the camp should be of equal status, and in this I was supported by the Advisory Committee which was formed soon after arrival, it was necessary to have some sort of machinery by which recalcitrance could be dealt with, for as things stood I might have the resounding title of Camp Leader but no authority went with it for keeping law and order. So it was suggested that a tribunal should be set up, the functions of which would be to hear cases of anti-social activity and the more serious complaints. The members, who would be appointed by popular, secret ballot, would pass their verdicts to the Camp Leader for action. There was little he could do by way of imposing punishment and, as I saw it, only four courses of action were open to him:

1. He could ask the Germans to deal with the culprit. (Imagine the reaction in the camp had he done this!).

2. He could issue a severe reprimand (which would do a fat lot of good!).

3. He could cut rations. (But as rations and nothing were about equal, that would have been inhumane).

4. He could impose extra fatigues. (This is what I did, but if any culprit refused to do them, I was back where I started).

To assist the Camp Leader and the tribunal, we formed a camp police. Though its members thought they would not have a difficult task when appointed, they soon discovered how mistaken they were. They tried every possible way to persuade the naughty boy to accept their authority, but here again, it needed only one man to complain to the German authorities that he was being ill-treated, for the Germans to begin interfering and we valued our small measure of self-government too highly to risk losing it.

In one particular case I was compelled to take action, and the results were most unfortunate for me.

The Americans complained that food was being stolen from them. After careful investigation, suspicion fell on one of our own people. The camp police approached the suspect and requested him to appear before the tribunal. He refused in the choicest terms. The tribunal then politely but firmly passed the buck to me.

Acting on the advice of the " wise men " of the camp, I sent the police with orders to arrest him and bring him in. They found him after a time and after some resistance he was brought to the camp office and I was informed of his arrival. Still believing that the friendly approach would be wisest, I issued an invitation to him to come in and talk the matter over quietly and reasonably. This being also refused, he was propelled into my office with a man-sized kick in the stern.

I asked everyone to leave us alone and began to talk to my guest in what I believed was a fatherly manner. I soon discovered that this was quite the wrong approach for informing me that I was an " under-sized, rat-faced basket " (only stronger), he began to advance on me in a most menacing manner. I retreated quickly before him and beat a tattoo on the wall to summon aid and my rescuers, led by Syd Jones, arrived only in the nick of time. It was quite obvious that I, the tribunal and the police were powerless to make any further move. In fact, in cases of open defiance of this kind, when the culprit was quite uninfluenced by public opinion, the Camp Leader was absolutely powerless unless he was prepared to resort to some sort of physical punishment illegally applied.

We had scarcely recovered from this open defiance and were still seeking ways and means to assert some sort of authority when another dangerous situation confronted us. In one particular room there were a number of " revolutionaries " who had plenty of time in which to work up a revolt. In the camp office we were aware that something was brewing, but where the storm-centre was located, who were involved or when it would happen, we could only guess. Fortunately we had friends in the room and late one evening we received a caller, Bill Arrowsmith, who brought us the urgent advice that trouble was about to begin.

The plan, apparently, was to set fire to a number of beds and gradually spread alarm and confusion throughout the whole camp. While this was going on a select number of trouble-makers were to search out the members of the camp office staff — us! — and the kitchen staff, and beat them up. (For the first time we learned that the basis of the grievances was an alleged unfair allocation of food, of which they believed themselves to be the only victims in the camp).

With visions of the camp being completely destroyed either by fire or wrecking, with German reprisals resulting, we decided to rally all available assistance and were lucky to be almost overwhelmed with offers of help. But while this was being organised, I went post-haste to the trouble area with the intention and hope of reasoning the so-termed revolutionaries out of their violent mood, or at least of limiting the trouble.

My arrival was undoubtedly a surprise and I could not have timed it better had I been in their innermost councils, for a Guy Fawkes meeting was in progress and I was able to establish at once the identity of the ring-leader. Without waiting to be introduced, I interrupted the meeting and before they could come to the attack, either verbally or physically, I launched into an address which, I feel sure, would have done credit to the Hon. Member for a certain constituency in South Wales. Giving them no chance to argue, I strongly condemned the folly of their ways and when I had finished I had swung the majority over to me. Though a small number of incorrigibles refused to take part, we concluded a truce and shook hands on it and I returned to the office realising that, despite my outspokenness, I was considerably shaken myself.

Nor were my brushes only with the internees. When the German staff had left the camp after their day's work, we were left in the charge of the officer of the military guard. As this unit was comprised of troops either recovering from wounds or resting before being returned to active service, the duty was only a temporary one and the personnel were therefore constantly changing.

Either through intent or wilful negligence, we had been subjected to a number of blackouts and as we had a number of old men among us, some of them very sick men, these black-outs were the cause of several accidents and considerable inconvenience. They also resulted in many complaints. As usual the senior was the " meat in the sandwich " and the Council of Room Seniors insisted that he should take a strong line with the Germans. The American section was even more emphatic about something being done and suggested that a complaint should be made to our Protecting Power.

The German camp office was sympathetic to me when I went down to see them about it and appreciated my difficulties. They assured me that strict orders had been given to the military that the mains were not to be switched off, provided that all the camp lights, with the exception of the hospital lights, were out in time. I have no doubt that this order was issued but it certainly failed in its object as one body of guards succeeded another.

The black-outs continued, and so did our protests, and with ever-increasing vigour. Finally, the American section put up such a concerted effort that the people living in the town outside the camp became alarmed, as they thought the internees had mutinied.

As strongly as possible the American senior, Harry McQuade, and I continued our efforts to gain satisfaction. We received the same assurances. At one time we thought we were really getting results, but it took a serious situation to cure the trouble for all time.

When once again we were subjected to a black-out, the British complement tried hard to be patient, but the Americans really went to town with pots and pans and achieved absolute pandemonium. Hoping to persuade them to be patient, too, and at the same time fearing that the Germans might take it into their heads to treat their behaviour as mutiny and begin shooting, I dashed over to their quarters and appealed to them to pipe down. I believed I had been successful and went back to our camp office, expecting by that time that a full-scale deputation of my own people would have found their way there with the aid of matches. In my haste I tripped over one of the old men, who told me that in trying to find his room he had fallen down some stone steps and injured himself. When I had found someone to help him, I speeded my return to the office.

As I reached the office an electric torch was flashed in my face and I was stopped by an armed guard. A German officer was shouting for the British "Lager Führer" and giving no one any chance to reply, and the office staff were receiving a real dressing down.

By this time I was so angry that I had made up my mind to settle this business of the black-outs once and for all. So I let the German officer have it and soon a shouting match in two languages had developed in full blast. To those within earshot it must have sounded like a rodeo.

By the time our vocabularies had run out, several doors were ajar and faces became distinguishable. Among them I noticed the Jewish camp doctor, Oshek, who spoke fluent German and asked him to come to my assistance in driving home my protest. He readily agreed to interpret for me and I believe that he gave an accurate rendering of what I said, for when I had finished the German officer flung his cape back over his shoulders with a flourish, and gave me the old one-two with trimmings, about-turned and marched off, followed by his escort, complete with torches and fixed bayonets.

Within a few minutes our electric light was restored and was greeted with loud cheers. From then on it seemed that our protest had been noted in the Wehrmacht records and we had no further trouble for a very long time.

All the members of the office staff suffered from delayed shock, myself not the least. When eventually we calmed down, it seemed to us like a fairy story with a happy ending. But at any rate it relieved us of a major headache.

When I reported to the German camp captain next morning, he at once commented on the incident and asked that in future I should be a little more civil to the officer of the guard. This worthy, he told me, though I have been unable to confirm it, was a relative of the late Kaiser, and a prince — not that I, or anyone to whom I told the story, was impressed.

The arrival of Red Cross parcels brightened our existence beyond belief. The food provided by the Germans was more or less disregarded, much of it being returned to the kitchens untouched.

But now that they ceased to be troubled by the demands of their stomach, everyone, almost without exception, began to turn their minds to other things, so that while we in the camp office were relieved of one problem, we found ourselves confronted with others. For what up to now had been secondary matters became matters of prime importance — walks outside the camp, fatigues, bed-bugs, letters, outside work and above all — NEWS!

The problem of outside work divided the camp and became the subject of bitter controversy even among the most level-headed. The main argument resolved itself into this: Were those who accepted work in the farms round about doing something of value for their fellow internees by preserving their own physical and mental fitness and giving their companions living space, or were they merely gaining the concession of limited freedom for themselves by working for our enemies? Put more simply, did the results which would obviously accrue to the well-being of the camp as a whole — from having a section of physically and mentally top-line inmates — justify the benefits which their work would undoubtedly bestow on the Germans?

When the German authorities first asked for volunteers for work on the farms, I strongly resisted their demand that I should submit their request to the camp. Naturally I consulted my helpers, and it was in my discussions with them that I realised I could not inflict my personal views on everybody and, indeed, began to doubt whether I had the right to do so. A meeting was called of all those interested in the project, to which the Germans sent a representative. This man gave the meeting a survey of the jobs open to us in the local factories producing non-essential war material, in sawmills and particularly on the farms.

I got up when he had sat down and said that I and the majority of my helpers were strongly opposed to the offer of work, and gave our reasons. By giving even the slightest assistance to the Germans in their food production, I said, we were helping to defeat the Allied blockade, which had already cost the lives of thousands of our own countrymen besides the heavy financial setback of many millions of pounds sterling. We considered that those who left the camp to work were acting contrary to our country's interests, since we could not see that the benefits of being occupied would amount to much except possibly for each individual concerned.

The meeting broke up after I had spoken and all agreed to sleep on the matter. I believe that what I had said weighed with a considerable number of internees, nevertheless, there were a number who accepted the German offer.

Though we felt a certain resentment against these men, we did appreciate the general comfort in living conditions which resulted from their exodus.

But I have slightly overrun my story, and must now go back a short way.

Chapter VII

FIRST CHRISTMAS IN CAPTIVITY

As I look back over these days, I become more and more convinced that the period from early November, 1942, to January, 1943, was one of the most significant periods of my life. And if I were asked to pick out the highlight of this period, I should say, without hesitation, Christmas, 1942, our first Christmas in captivity.

Though we were by no means free of trouble, by mid-December, 1942, two months after we had arrived at the Schloss, life in the camp had settled down very well. In this short space of time we had been able to devise, and put into operation, a workmanlike arrangement which was designed to give the greatest benefits to every single member in the camp. Birth, rank, position and fortune for the time being had lost all significance, and the principle of absolute equality for all the inmates was accepted by all — or nearly all. There were a number of ex-officers who still used their ranks and these held that since their commissions came direct from the Crown, it was infra dig for them to be classed with the masses. For the time being, however, they were overruled. On this basis, camp duties were shared by all who were physically fit, regardless of whether they were retired colonels or sewage men temporarily separated from their jobs. If a man wanted to share in the food — then the all-important problem — he must share the responsibilities of camp life, provided his body or mind did not handicap him. There was among us, fortunately, a good doctor, an Irishman who had once served in the R.A.M.C., who knew a would-be lead-swinger as soon as he set eyes on him, and would stand no nonsense. To be quite fair, there were exceptionally few who tried to pull a fast one, though, of course, there was the usual number of moaners.

When Christmas began to loom up, therefore, we were pretty well organised and able to turn our attention to making preparations for this festival which means so much to the Englishman.

In our Red Cross store there was a quantity of biscuits and condensed milk, which had been sent into the camp by a neighbouring British officers' camp immediately they had heard on the bush-telegraph that a number of their countrymen had arrived at the Schloss and were having to exist, for the time being, on German rations. It was a gesture and a kindness which, I am sure, was deeply appreciated by ninety-nine point nine per cent of us.

We were keeping these supplies for an emergency, but I believed that we should be justified in using part of them to add a touch to the season which, in the state we were in, did not promise to be very festive. When I put my idea to the camp office staff, Deputy Roy Skingle, Len Collins, Don Campbell, Secretaries, and Jock Campbell as chief cook and bottle washer, and the stores staff, they agreed, and we decided to bring up a sufficient supply, after lights out, to give each member of the camp a small Christmas treat. As the Germans held the key to the stores, we had to ask their permission, which was granted.

I cannot say that getting up before dawn on Christmas morning in the freezing cold was hard work for my helpers and me, for we thoroughly enjoyed being able to play Father Christmas. Every man in the camp, British and American, was allocated one tin of milk and one packet of biscuits.

As we went into each room we shouted: "Wakey, wakey! Here comes Father Christmas!" and then sang a carol, chosen with care and appropriate to the types we were visiting. Then we went from bunk to bunk distributing the British officers' gift and shaking hands and wishing everyone Happy Christmas. It was natural, I suppose, that the first room we awakened from their slumbers at this unearthly hour should have considered they might well have been left until last, but when we told them we had come to them first because we were afraid stocks might run out, and that they could consider themselves lucky to be still in bed, because it was extremely cold, all was well.

The reason I said 99.9 per cent of the camp's inmates were grateful to the British officers for their gift is because of something that happened to us, which brought us to a full-stop with a considerable jolt. After two hours of distributing our two gifts, filled with the importance of our own verbosity and the exhilaration of our Father Christmas rôle, we came upon one internee whose liver had obviously turned sour on him in the night and who told me in no uncertain terms exactly what I could do with the milk and biscuits. Further, he flatly refused to shake hands with any so-and-so, or with any of so-and-so's so-and-so stooges, and nothing we could say or do could make him change his mind. He certainly deflated our ego. However, little by little we recovered our spirits and by the time we got back to the camp office, his ears must almost have caught fire, so freely was his attitude discussed.

After morning church attendance the camp office staff went to pay our respects and take our gifts to the Americans. We were all deeply touched by the sincere welcome we received. These men, who came from Luxembourg, Belgium, Norway, Yugoslavia, Czechoslovakia, France, Germany and Greece, and other countries I forget, spoke to us through interpreters and shared their meagre rations with us in the true spirit of Christmas.

But if we were touched by their welcome then, it was nothing to the emotion we felt when a party of 20 American Greeks, including an American archaeologist, Charles House, who had been trapped in Greece by the German invasion, invited the camp staff to tea on New Year's Day. The archaeologist brought the message and we readily and grate-fully accepted.

The party was not memorable for the quality or quantity of the fare provided, but I for one will never forget the entertainment they put on. This consisted of Greek songs and dances to the accompaniment of an accordion.

Midway through the party one of them who, judging by his age and dignity, was a senior, stood up and addressed me — in Greek — as the British camp senior. At the end of his speech, of which none of us had understood a word but got the meaning nevertheless, I was asked to receive a hand-painted banner about two feet by one and a half feet, on which were painted the flags of our two countries, with suitable wording in Greek extolling the undying friendship of Britain and Greece.

When I think of the bitterness which rages between our two countries over Cyprus as I write these words, I

86

reflect on that little ceremony in Laufen internment camp during World War II and surely, I say, there must be something the ordinary man can offer which might help countries in time of disagreement? Having lived in a small island for a number of years, with its resulting limited outlook, the whole experience of living and mixing daily with men of other nations was one of the most valuable things to come out of our misfortune. It certainly advanced my own education considerably. I came to the conclusion that it is most silly to take a dislike to, or imagine a hatred for, any individual because they happen to come from a country whose leaders are so-and-so. It seemed to me that only by getting to know them on a basis of equality can you, or they, decide whether you, or they, are fit and proper persons to live with. (Believe me, among the British internees we had a few real stinkers, whom we would readily have swopped). On the wider and more intriguing field of international politics it is surely tragic that nothing has apparently been gained from the many contacts between men from strange lands who had no motive more ulterior than friendship.

After leaving our hosts we visited the staffs of the several departments such as the kitchen, Red Cross stores, Post Office, laundry, dry rations, hospital and hygiene, to express our thanks for their splendid help. It was only at the end of the day, when we were having our nightly chat in our bunks, that we realised how fortunate we were to have so much to occupy our minds. We had had a very full Christmas season of unique experiences which had done much to counter our loss of freedom and the continual longing for a re-union with our loved ones after nearly three years.

It has always been my great regret that during a police raid on the camp, quite by accident I destroyed the banner, together with several other personal notes, by burning them.

Chapter VIII

LIFE IMPROVES A LITTLE

I HAVE ALREADY MADE A BRIEF reference to the changes which the arrival of the Red Cross food parcels brought into our lives. The first arrived in January, 1943, and this event was certainly a major turning point in our existence. The Germans, however, seemed to resent anything which might make us more comfortable and according either to the mood of the local commandant, or to superior orders, they set out to take as much edge off our joy as they could.

Sometimes the parcels would be delivered to us complete, but with every tin pierced by the German staff. Once they insisted on the extremely unpleasant method — used chiefly in the P.O.W. camps as a reprisal after a mass escape — of emptying all the contents of the parcel out of the tins into a single receptacle. The result of this was disastrous for not only had the food to be eaten quickly before it went bad, but it took considerable patience to sort out the various contents, if this was possible, for raspberry jam, pilchards, dried fruit, condensed milk, sugar, oats, tinned meat, margarine, and whatever else the parcel contained, were all mixed in one indescribable mess. I believe that some of the men did not even attempt to separate the different commodities, but mixed the lot thoroughly and then, having made themselves comfortable in case of sudden illness, closed their eyes and dug in.

Fortunately, this happened only once. We were told that it had been done to give us second thoughts in case any of us was thinking of escaping. Escapes were few and far between. The most successful remained at liberty only a few days. Once a rather sick man attempted to scale the barbed wire, got his clothing caught up, and was lucky not to be shot while attempting to escape. His effort resulted in the whole camp being punished by the Germans withdrawing the use of a small island which was linked to the main camp by a wooden footbridge. The island was important to us because we conducted our sports there.

Our mail began to arrive regularly now and this made a tremendous difference to us mentally. Besides the food parcels, the Red Cross sent us clothing, which was also greatly appreciated.

The German defeat at Stalingrad at the end of January, 1943, also worked in our favour. When we had come among them in the previous September, the Germans, flushed with victory, had been very cock-a-hoop and had treated us with scorn and derision. If they were not yet actually aware that this defeat was the beginning of the end for them, something happened inside them to soften them up in their treatment of us. Perhaps they were not aware what they were doing, but in effect they were trying to improve their own situation when the day of final reckoning came: "We've treated you quite well, so we can expect consideration from you."

For us, Stalingrad, like El Alamein had been, was a signal for confidence. Since it coincided with the improvement in our physical condition, we took great heart from it.

By the spring of 1943, our situation had indeed improved so much that even the camp office staff was in danger of becoming bored with routine. This led to an escapade, the merits of which I still seriously doubt. It was put into our heads, I think, by the visits we began to receive after the tide had begun to turn, from the various German Commands who wished to know if we were happy, if the food was sufficient, if we were getting enough exercise, and so on.

During a period in which we were feeling particularly browned off, a member of the staff, Roy Skingle, who, in stature and colouring, was not unlike the "beloved" Führer, obtained some make-up and clothing which transformed him, we thought, into Adolf's twin. Delighted with this new diversion from the habitual bridge, ludo and heated discussions of the qualities of certain female film stars, we decided to present our "Führer" to one of the camp doctors, who was a Jew. I told the doctor that I was expecting a German of high rank and believed him to be already in the camp. Having put the final touches to our "Führer," I knocked at the doctor's door, called him to attention and stood aside to admit "Adolf," who gave the doctor the old one-two sign and then, with solemn face, presented him with an Iron Cross expertly made from a Klim tin. Before the doctor could recover from his first shock, the procession withdrew. When I returned to the doctor's office after a short time, he was only then just beginning to return to normal and I felt very ashamed of myself for making him the victim of our joke. However, when he had fully recovered, he took it in good part and we became good friends. Later, he would recall the incident with great good humour.

Our success with the doctor prompted us to present our "Führer" to others and we next visited a room which housed 40 men. Halting outside the selected room, we crowded round "Adolf" to shield him from the view of any German who might unexpectedly turn up. Then I entered the room and called the men, some of whom were sleeping, some playing cards or reading, to attention. I announced that the Führer was taking a personal interest in our welfare and visiting us in person. "Adolf" responded splendidly, took note of certain details, addressed me in his best guttural "German," to which I replied through an interpreter, and then he called for another Iron Cross. This, made from cardboard, was carried in ceremoniously on a cushion and, with much heel-clicking, "Adolf" presented it to the man who had most loudly advocated internees taking jobs outside the camp. Amid loud "Sieg Heils" the party then retreated and it wasn't until we had laughed our heads off in the camp office that reason suddenly returned and it struck me how silly we, and particularly I, had been.

The danger of our impersonation was brought home to us within a few hours. The camp postmen—internees Bill Boalch and Boley Pittard—found in the German mail box a letter addressed to the Camp Commandant. (The German mail box was used for addressing personal requests to the authorities). When we opened the letter we found it contained, in printed characters, a full account of our impersonation. Who the stooge was we never discovered, but the letter's falling into our hands was a lucky break for us. For several weeks thereafter we kept a very close watch on all outgoing mail, and only after the passing of some time without any reaction from the Germans did the tension relax and we began to breathe normally. All mention of impersonation was strictly taboo, and the only excuse for the ridiculous episode that I can offer is that extreme boredom undermines the sanity of internees. Of that there is no shadow of doubt.

To brighten up life a little, several shows were staged by the more versatile of our members, under Padre Gerhold, Entertainments Officer. With the help of make-up provided by the Y.M.C.A., we were able to produce quite a number of attractive " females." One show in which all the cast were " females " particularly attracted attention. Previous efforts had brought only half-full houses, but for this the House Full notices were displayed a whole hour before the curtain went up. One of the cast, Dennis Bond, looked so desirable that he was saved from molestation only by the strong-arm action of the specially reinforced Camp Police, under Syd Jones. Afterwards the unfortunate chap was so pestered for dates that he never again appeared on the stage.

I have already mentioned that we had a sports ground on an island just outside the camp confines. Here we had a football pitch about one-third the normal size. During the wet season it was transformed into a shallow bath, as it had steep sides and the drainage, I imagine, was non-existent. When it froze in winter the pitch turned into a skating rink. Nevertheless, it was a great asset to us and to be deprived of it was a great punishment for all; for not only did it mean so much to the footballers, but those who were too old or did not wish to play also used it as a walking ground [See plate 3].

It matters not in which part of the world or whatever the circumstances, the natives of Jersey and Guernsey must at some time resort to an argument about something. Although we were united while " in the bag " and working extremely well together, we could not forget that great occasion in peace time when one island had trounced the other at some particular sport. So even in our restricted circumstances insular fervour found expression at some sporting event. Other members of our camp were at a loss to understand this temporary lapse in unity.

The great sporting event was the soccer Muratti, and for days prior to the match the merits of each team kept the camp alive [See plate 1]. The respective selection committees came under severe criticism; unfortunately for them, as they were always "on tap" they could not escape personal contact with their critics. On the great day the teams were given glamour treatment and a pre-match practice was enhanced by photographs. Within the space of minutes torrential rain came and washed out the carefully made markings, then threatened to submerge the pitch. By the time the storm had passed the ground was under several inches of water and all hands turned-to in an effort to bale out. The raised banks which enclosed three sides made natural drainage extremely slow.

Having cleared the water to the satisfaction of the referee the battle was declared on, with a delayed starting time, and early arrivals started to take up vantage points equipped wtih any utensil with which they could make a noise, and sporting the colours of their favourites.

The appearance of the teams was greeted with the maximum volume of noise. The inhabitants of Laufen might well have wondered if they were housing a camp of mentally defective internees, while the German guard was promptly reinforced. As the ball was often booted over the wire into the river which ran on either side they proved useful in fishing it out. One guard over-reached and took a neat header into the river amid loud cheers from the internees. He was rescued by his fellow guards, but his error of judgment had cost us a football so he had little sympathy from us.

The referee and linesmen were presented to the rival captains with due pomp, and as they already knew each other only too well the crowd started to become impatient for the expected mud bath.

To win the toss meant little advantage as the crowd on the raised banks kept any wind from entering the pocket-sized pitch, but at least the winner could choose the end with the least flood water.

As the goalkeeper for the green-and-whites—the Guernsey colours—I had to defend a goal of about eight feet wide by seven feet high, in view of its size this seemed quite easy, but when you took into account that every moment of play you were facing attack, as even from goalkicks you were often called upon to save while harassed by the opposing forward line of three death or glory boys who were receiving inspiration from the line, the task was by no means easy.

Everything was scaled down to one-third size, but with teams of seven, three forwards, a roving half-back, two backs and the goalkeeper, and long before half-time it was impossible to distinguish friend from foe.

During the interval a short tactical talk took place, and as we were now about to kick into the tide of flood water on the left flank it was suggested that our winger be equipped with an aqualung; however, the referee would not agree to this innovation.

Again after half-time the rain came down in bucketfuls. Play continued though the support dwindled until only those in doubtful state of mind remained to cheer the teams on. The game deteriorated due to the conditions, and free-kicks were plentiful.

As the result of an underwater foul a penalty was awarded against us and as the "spot" could not be identified the ball was placed on an atoll of mud and the penalty kicker withdrew into deep water preparatory to taking his run-up. As the "keeper" I had always found that on a dry day it was extremely difficult to keep from personal injury when facing a penalty, as the goals were small and the "keeper" was used as a target. However, this penalty seemed different as it was doubtful if the ball could be cleared from the mud sufficiently to reach me with any force.

Such were the wiles of the opposition that the kick was executed in a kind of scoop action which lobbed the ball —and surrounding mud—into the air, and the whole reached me simultaneously, with the result that by looking upwards for the ball I received a shower of mud in my eyes. The ball hit the crossbar and rebounded on to the back of my head and into the goal, amid cheers from the opposition.

Having received trainer service to remove the mud from my eyes, play continued and in the dying minutes the game was saved by a spectacular goal, to score which our forward line united in a feint attack which left the ball submerged, for our half-back to retrieve and dribble into goal while the bewildered opposition concentrated elsewhere.

The result was a draw and as extra time was considered to be courting pneumonia it was mutually agreed to replay when conditions improved. As this match also resulted in a draw the honour was shared.

The only other place to walk was known as the " Bird Cage." This was a small circular path surrounding a patch of grass. When the island was forbidden to us, and all the camp was exercising, it resembled Piccadilly Circus on Mafeking victory night. As the cold weather called for a brisk pace to prevent the blood from freezing in one's veins, going round and round in this closed circuit quickly made one giddy [See plate 4].

The use of the concert hall was dependent on the weather—its roof leaked badly—or on the mood of the Germans. Even so we came to appreciate it highly.

Then there was our swimming pool. When the Germans first announced that we could use the swimming pool, I visualised an up-to-date bath, situated outside the camp in a place which we could not see from any of our look-out posts. But when I was conducted to what we at once christened " The Puddle," I found a kind of cistern measuring roughly 20 feet by 12 feet and possibly five feet deep. In the hot summer weather anyone entering it did so at serious risk of never coming out again, so great would be the crush. Then it could be likened to a fisherman's net, full of fishes fighting in their death-struggles. More than one internee was dragged out of it more dead than alive.

What sport meant to us I am quite unable to evaluate. I do know that the morale would have deteriorated so badly without it that all discipline would have gone by the board. We inmates of Laufen owe a great debt to the Y.M.C.A. After having to be content to kick around a tin, it was a great joy receiving a very generous supply of sporting equipment of all kinds from the Y.M.C.A. Now, all who wished to play football, handball, table tennis, quoits or rugby or keep fit with the punch ball or boxing gloves, could do so.

With the arrival of the equipment, sports could be put on an organised basis. Various teams were formed and a competitive spirit soon developed. Naturally, the representatives of Jersey and Guernsey wanted to stage a trial of strength and many fine games of rugby and soccer took place, with the honours evenly shared. The 'pièce de resistance' was the rugby challenge match between Great Britain and the U.S.A. Several beds were set aside in the hospital for emergencies and the whole camp lined the pitch.

Spot—faithful friend

Inter-island trophy presentation

Plate 1

Feldkommandantur 515   Jersey, den 18. Sept. 1942

    Frank Edward Stroobant,
    3,Doyle Terrace,Doyle Road,
    St.Peter - Port.

Sie haben sich auf Grund der Bekanntmachung der Feldkommandantur 515 vom 15.9.1942 am 23.9.42 um 12 Uhr in einzufinden.	On account of the Notice of the Feldkommandantur 515 dated Sept.15th, 1942 you have to report yourself / yourselves at on Sept.23rd.42 in Gaumont Cinema
Es ist mitzunehmen die vorliegende Aufforderung nebst persoenlichen Ausweispapieren.	You have to take with you this order together with papers proving your identity.
Die Mitnahme warmer Kleidung, fester Stiefel, etwas ~unavorrat, Essgeschirr, Trinkbecher und moeglichst einer Decke ist notwendig. Des Gepaeck ~arf nicht schwerer sein als Sie es tragen koennen und ist mit einem Zettel mit Ihrer ~ ~anschrift zu versehen.	It is necessary that you fit yourself / yourselves out with warm clothes, solid boots, some provisions, meal-dishes, drinking-bowl, and, if possible, a blanket. Your luggage must not be heavier than you can carry and must bear a label with ~ full address.
Ferner wird anheimgestellt, pro Person einen verschlossenen Koffer mit Kleidungsstuecken ~ur Nachsendung bereitzustellen. Auf dem Koffer ist genaue Anschrift anzubringen.	It is left to you to get, for each person, a trunk ready packed with clothes and locked for shipment to you. You must mark your full address on each trunk.
Es wird ferner freigestellt Geld im Betrage bis zu RM 10.- in Reichskreditkassenscheinen pro Person mitzunehmen.	It is also left to you to take with you an amount of money up to Reichsmarks 10.- in German notes of Reichskreditkassen for each person.
Falls Sie dieser Aufforderung nicht nachkommen, haben Sie kriegsgerichtliche Bestra~ung zu gewaertigen.	Should you fail to obey this order, you must expect to be punished by a martial court.

Der Fel ~mmandant:

gez ~ckfuss

THE CONTROLLING COMMITTEE OF THE STATES OF GUERNSEY.

    Re: Feldkommandantur Order dated 15th September, 1942,
        relating to British Subjects.

Received of _Frank Edward Stroobant._

Address _3 Doyle Terrace_

Identity No. _3333._

Declaration of his family of _Seif_ persons.

Date _18. 9. 42_   Signature _R Golding_

Plate 2   Marching orders!

Plate 3

The Rugby Football Side

Morning Parade

Plate 4

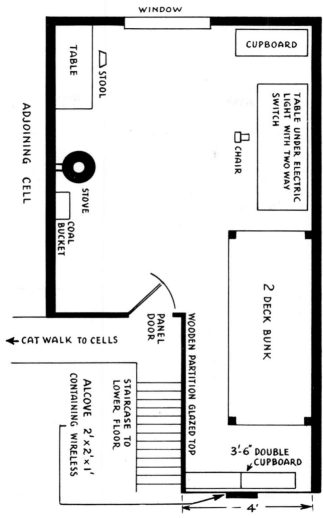

Plate 5

Plan of my cell

GABLE WALL OF BUILDING

WINDOW

CUPBOARD

TABLE UNDER ELECTRIC LIGHT WITH TWO WAY SWITCH

CHAIR

TABLE

STOOL

STOVE

COAL BUCKET

ADJOINING CELL

PANEL DOOR

WOODEN PARTITION GLAZED TOP

2 DECK BUNK

← CAT WALK TO CELLS

STAIRCASE TO LOWER FLOOR.

ALCOVE 2'x2'x1' CONTAINING WIRELESS

3'-6" DOUBLE CUPBOARD

4'

The Author, Billy Williams and the Forbidden Whisper.

Plate 6

Smolensk

Plate 7

Exhibits at Katyn. The author is the only civilian in this picture

Plate 8

Among the American team were several types who, to say the least, were rugged. They claimed to have played football before in the States and I for one, before the opening whistle, was prepared to accept this broad statement. As soon as play started, I realised why they play football in America wearing everything barring the kitchen sink. From the word go the game rapidly developed into something like the slaughter of the innocents. The referee, Douggie Marshall, was quite unable to assert his authority, though I doubt very much if it would have made any difference had he been able to do so.

As the game progressed, the standard declined. During a line-out it was fatal to wait for the ball to come into play, and after the first line-out, during which our pack got slapped down like nine-pins, it was every man for himself. My opposite number produced several rules I had never seen written down in any book, and after a number of bone-shattering tackles, I left someone else to look after him. I had only one thought in mind: When would the whistle go for no side? Surely the referee's watch must have stopped.

But the game went on and the forces of Great Britain were rallied by Padre Gerhold, who was skippering the side. Only because he inspired me did I stay on the field. I have a faint suspicion that my feelings were shared by all, with the exception of the skipper himself, who literally returned blow for blow. Once he had secured the ball and had started to move forward, he seemed to tuck his knees up under his chin and plough through regardless.

The final score was U.S.A. seven points, Great Britain six points. When asked how he had arrived at the final figure, the referee was unable to give a satisfactory answer, but assured us that from his point of view it was a most satisfactory result, as without doubt the Americans deserved the victory. At the end of the game there were hearty mutual congratulations and our opponents wanted to know when we would play the return match, as they were sure we should win next time. As far as I was concerned there was no next time because I had used every excuse to save my skin.

Many of the Guernsey contingent in the camp were still appreciative of the great efforts which the States of Guernsey had made to give them the very best that was available at the time of the deportation, and several of them had made suggestions that some way of repaying the kindness should be found. In the spring of 1943 we learned that it was possible to send money from Laufen to certain charities back in the island. For those who wished to contribute, arrangements were made with German co-operation for a sum named by the subscriber to be withdrawn from his bank account—if it would stand it—and paid into a central fund organised by Charles Daniels. In this way we were able to show our appreciation by donating more than £200 to Guernsey charities, while Jersey charities similarly benefited from donations by our fellow internees from that island. But it meant much more to us than being able partially to repay a kindness. In some way it seemed to draw us closer to the island and to make us feel that we were not entirely cut off.

Another improvement which helped to cheer us up in the spring of 1943 was the permission granted to small parties of internees to go on conducted walking tours in the surrounding countryside. The elderly men in particular appreciated this concession, since they were precluded by their age from taking part in the more vigorous and violent forms of exercise. Not only that, the country around us was very beautiful and the guards were usually men from the district who were proud to show off their homeland, and the change of scenery provided a valuable stimulant.

We had in the camp a number of cases requiring specialised treatment. Up to this time this had been refused on one pretext or another, as a general rule, but now they were admitted to Salzburg hospital. The patients who went to Salzburg were full of praise for the highly-skilled and kindly way in which they were looked after. In some cases, when a serious operation or a long stay in hospital for treatment was necessary, regular visits from the Camp Senior or a special friend were arranged. Almost all the visitors were favourably impressed with what they saw, and we were all grateful to the doctors and nurses who, in true conformity with the ethics of their professions, did not allow the fact that we were enemy nationals to affect their humanitarianism.

A similar tribute is also due to the doctors and staff of the mental hospital in Salzburg. Unhappily, one or two of our number were unable to stand the strain of internment but in the mental hospital they received sympathetic care, as those who were permitted to visit them could testify.

As part of the new policy, those of us who wished were allowed to go out of camp, under guard, to do tree-felling and logging in the nearby Austrian forest. Every evening they would bring back to the Schloss the fruits of their labour, which assured that we should not go cold for lack of fuel. A regular supply of peat was also sent in when we produced workers for the peat fields. Without these two supplies of fuel to eke out the meagre coal ration we should have suffered considerably, and the efforts of the volunteers ought to have been appreciated more than they were.

Several of us were later to have good reason to realise how fortunate we were to experience the change of policy, and to have the food and clothing sent by the Red Cross, and the sports and scholastic equipment provided by the Y.M.C.A.

When we were eventually liberated by the Americans we were asked to supply volunteers to assist the nursing staff at the local hospital to which a number of the prisoners from a nearby notorious concentration camp had been taken after being freed, in the faint hope of saving their lives. Those of us who went to do what we could, found only living skeletons. It amazed us that life could still exist within those frames, on which skin like parchment was stretched tightly from one bone to another, and every bone threatened to burst through at the least pressure. With the skilled medical aid which was given them, and to a very much lesser degree with the inexpert nursing we were able to give them, it was possible to save several of this tragic company. But how it brought home to us the insignificance of our own trials and sufferings, which we had believed to be great!

We had not received the barbaric treatment which they had received. Though we had been hungry, very hungry indeed in the early days, at least we had had sufficient food of excellent quality to keep our bones well clothed with flesh, and this only increased our debt of gratitude to the Red Cross.

When I cottoned on to the change in the attitude of our captors toward us, and after a time saw that they were not just a flash in the pan, I was prompted to put two suggestions to the Germans. First was that the unfit men should be repatriated, and the second that the camp would appreciate a wireless set on which they might listen to the B.B.C. news.

Neither of these suggestions found favour, as was expected, but we did find a way of getting round the problem of being cut off from information of what was going on in the world outside, information which we could trust and which helped to keep up our spirits.

Chapter IX

FORBIDDEN WHISPER

THOUGH WE WERE NOT TREATED with brutality; though thanks to the Red Cross, from the time they contacted us we suffered little from lack of food; though we could keep ourselves occupied with the equipment sent us by the Y.M.C.A., we still lacked the most important thing to give us real peace of mind—NEWS, real, true NEWS. We were not entirely cut off from all knowledge of what was going on outside for we were fed with German radio reports, Lord Haw-Haw's fulminations and, sometimes, we were provided with German newspapers. But we knew we could not trust the information which the club-footed Dr. Josef Goebbels decided we could be told, and consequently there was a big trade in rumours, which varied from the sublime to the ridiculous, but which only served to keep our nerves and minds on edge.

We had often discussed the subject and had always come to the conclusion that if we went much longer without authentic news, some of us would go completely round the bend. But there was nothing that we could think of that would remedy our want. There was no one among us who could make a wireless set and in any case even if there had been we could not have secured the necessary parts and, finally, there was no one who could be our "sparks."

In 1943 I lost my job as Camp Senior. I may as well confess that I had been trying to lose it before my trip to Russia—which I will describe in the next chapter—and even more so since my return, when I found that certain sections of the camp believed that I had gone pro-German.

It all arose out of my trying to be far-sighted. Rightly or wrongly, I wanted to maintain an adequate stock of Red Cross parcels in the camp so that we should not be short of food during the coming winter which, if it turned out to be anything like the previous one, would be far more rigorous than we were used to. In my view, an increase in Allied bombing was a certainty. There was a distinct possibility of a second front being opened. Both these would undoubtedly cause a certain amount of chaos to the German lines of communication and since we were some way from the source of supply, it was more than possible, in the circumstances, that the parcels would not arrive as regularly as they had done up to now.

My plan was that instead of each man receiving one complete parcel every week, he should be given one only every 14 days; alternatively, that two men should share a weekly parcel. The parcels which would be saved in this way would then hold against a possible future rainy day.

Having made my theory known, I sat back to await the howls of protest which I was sure would come. I had not long to wait. Within an hour or two I was brought a petition signed by the Room Seniors demanding a meeting with me to discuss the plan. Naturally, their wish was my command, and we met in solemn conclave. I re-stated, perhaps more forcibly than I had done before, exactly what was in my mind, and met with the strongest opposition. When all had aired their views, a vote was taken and it went overwhelmingly against me. Had I made no move myself, I think I should have been ousted from the camp leadership anyway and, realising this, I took the bull by the horns and tendered my resignation, which was accepted. I heaved a great sigh of relief.

In fact, my theory proved wrong, as no shortage of food parcels occurred.

The office staff seemed to mourn my departure, possibly working on the theory that "the devil you know is better than the devil you don't know." The new senior, Ambrose Sherwill, was a splendid man who brought to his post all the dignity I lacked and because of it became known to the American section as "Horsehead."

Being now an ordinary, unofficial member of the camp, I was at the same time now "homeless" for I could no longer claim the right to a bed in the Senior's office-cum-living-room-cum-bedroom-cum-washroom.

My plight was resolved for me, however, by Joe Everett, the camp dentist, agreeing to take me into his two-bunk room, though only after some protestations. As dentist he received certain preferential treatment which included living in a room by himself, if he wished.

When I had moved in I began to look for a suitable job. My temperament is such I must always be doing something. I do not enjoy leisure unless it is filled with physical activity. I also wanted to continue being of some service to my fellow internees.

I still spent my evenings in the camp office, chiefly to keep an eye on the large credit balance of Camp Marks I had earned at bridge, rummy and sevens. I strongly opposed the suggestion that now, as I was only a visitor, the slate should be wiped clean for a new start.

The new Camp Senior had decided not to leave his present room, the House of Lords, and move into the camp office, so the party for the evening sessions was the same as before, and as before, our conversation centred on the lack of news. It was, we decided, gradually becoming soul-destroying. We knew that something must be done, and done as quickly as possible, since some of the older men, in particular, were losing all interest in life, and just roamed around aimlessly, or slept the time away. This was summer, so what would it be like in winter?

Though we felt that we were probably driving up against a stone wall, we sought the opinions of carefully selected men whom we knew could be trusted absolutely, as to the possibility of building a wireless receiving set and whether, once having built it, we could operate and maintain it. These enquiries produced a very ingenious character from Jersey, Billy Williams, who was confident that he could build a set provided he could " borrow " the necessary parts. He lost no time in sounding the possibilities and next day volunteered for the work in a local radio store. In a very short space of time the parts began to arrive in the camp. Our expert had either concealed them attached to various parts of his body, or they were secreted in the incoming bundles of internee laundry from the outside laundry, a method which had the unconscious protection of the German guard.

Possession of the parts then raised three important problems for us. Where would it be reasonably safe to build the set? Where would it be reasonably safe to operate the set once it had been built? Who was going to run the set if it ever worked?

Now my room mate, the dentist, had only been let into the secret when one day he had found a length of wire hidden in the toes of his spare shoes. He protested strongly about being involved in anything so risky and for a time the parts had to be redistributed and progress was held up. Sad to relate, he fell ill, which necessitated his urgent removal to Salzburg hospital. This left me in sole occupation of the room and so I was able to provide a solution to all three of our problems.

The parts arrived with such regularity and frequency that we had difficulty in finding safe hiding places for them. By the beginning of November, 1943, our expert decided that he had all he needed for a start to be made on the construction.

Before we began, we thought it necessary to have a working team of three. To avoid raising any suspicion among the Germans by having one or more members of the camp office staff absent from their duties for an unreasonable length of time we co-opted an outsider. This was a young Jerseyman, Bill Drinkwater, who, before the war, had been training as a Jesuit. On arrival at the camp he had been a quiet, intellectual type with deep religious convictions and if his contact with the mixed bunch of men in his room did not help his studies, at least it broadened his outlook. Before we had finished with him his views on life in general were much broader still and he also had a good working knowledge of the English language as used by the working classes. Having accepted our invitation to join the team, he was duly initiated as " solder melter and stoker."

I have little mechanical knowledge of any sort and certainly not about radio, so my chief contribution was providing the room for the work and allowing the room's allocation of fuel to be used for the ultimate benefit of the camp. The work-room was situated on the top floor of the cell building, popularly known as the laundry building. (Reference to the plan on plate 5 will help to understand my description of it). At some time in the past it could well have been used as the guard-room for the adjoining cells.

At the end of the room there was a long, narrow kind of alcove which just took the two-tier bunk, the effect of which was to provide more space than would be found in other rooms on the cell floor.

As soon as construction work started, the Genius was out on his own. We merely said "Yes" or "No," sometimes in the wrong order. When the work was almost half completed, my room mate returned from Salzburg still a sick man, and his condition was not helped when he became acquainted with what was going on. On the pretext of having a weak heart, which prevented his climbing the stairs, he moved his bed and possessions to his surgery, having obtained the sanction of the German doctor to do so. This solved what might well have been a very difficult situation.

One of the major security problems was the matter of securing the door, as no keys were allowed, and the door itself was not very strong. Finally, we devised a method by jamming a tin-opener in such a position that the handle would not move even under heavy pressure. The problem of where to keep the set while it was being made, and a safe hiding place for it afterwards, solved itself.

Directly behind the 3ft. 6in. double locker we found a ready-made recess, 2ft. by 1ft., which was an ideal spot and had indeed, we eventually learned, been used for just this purpose by former officer inmates from the Polish Army.

As the set progressed, piece by piece, there seemed to be a good deal of trial and error about it. Occasionally the Genius gave vent to his wrath by abusing us, his two stooges. On one particular occasion, at an apparently vital juncture, the soldering iron was in continuous demand and we were compelled to burn three of my bedboards to keep the stove sufficiently hot. Even this failed to satisfy the maestro, who greatly enlarged the vocabulary of the "solder melter and stoker" as he gave way to his rage. As a matter of fact, we did not receive quite the undivided attention and support of the Quiet One that we had anticipated. There were periods when he seemed to go off into a world of his own, and then the fire would go out. This, and other failings, resulted in our renaming him "Datas" after the famed memory man; and later he annoyed us considerably by becoming engrossed in the life story of Cleopatra and, later, of Jean Harlow, so far had his education advanced, to the detriment of his work. This last lapse nearly cost him his job!

One of our expert's biggest headaches was getting hold of a transformer, an absolutely vital part, apparently, since without it the set would not work. He found the answer after much searching. He was acting as maintenance engineer for the German-controlled Camp radio and also the set in the guard room and at times was called in to do repair work on them. On one such occasion, he put the guard room set out of commission and on the pretext of its requiring major repairs, took it away to work on it. He then reported that the transformer was "kaput" and that a replacement would be required.

How he worked it I don't know, but the fact remains that one evening he returned to camp with the precious transformer secreted on his body, an act calling for a high degree of courage, because it was not a small piece. Although it solved our problem, it delayed the return of the German guard set indefinitely and, in the end, they asked for and received a replacement from Munich.

Every detail of the work was explained to us, the two stooges, with great care. We were told to make mental notes in case we should have to make our own sets when this one was worn out in, say, 10 years' time, when he no longer expected to be among us! But it was not much good, for neither of us could understand even the most simple technical or, for that matter, non-technical terms.

Nor did the work progress uninterrupted and without scares. The camp office was always a source of prompt information, however, if anything unusual was likely to happen and we managed to avoid the worst dangers. Now and again our door would be tried by mistake and the curious individual would probably go away wondering how we had contrived to lock it and why we wanted to lock it. On the whole, though, it did not go too badly. One of my tasks, among those one-handed jobs I was given to do after lights out, was rewinding the transformer. This necessitated my keeping an accurate record of each 100 turns of wire I made round a coil. Having made probably 20,000 turns according to instructions, the expert would most likely decide there were too many and I would have to undo it all. There were times when I positively disliked the Genius.

At long last the transformer was ready except for the fitting of the baffle plates, and the last of these proved very obstinate. In trying to get it into place, the Genius damaged the winding of the coils and I had to do the work all over again. This time there was no trouble and the Genius announced that the set "should go now."

We decided to christen our baby officially, and those who had conspired with us were invited to the ceremony, for which the expert had smuggled in two bottles of fire-water. That night two important things happened, I accepted the set and named it the Forbidden Whisper; and the Quiet One slipped further into the morass of life by acquiring a taste for fire-water [See plate 6].

During the manufacturing stage, out of sheer bravado I had offered to build a suitable cabinet for the set and in a surge of enthusiasm had declared that it would be an expert job, with the ends dove-tailed. I failed very badly and when the finished article was shown that evening, the cabinet was the object of scorn. By that time, however, I had become hardened to all forms of abuse and the unkind remarks ran off me like water off a duck's back.

When all the fire-water had been disposed of, the christening party broke up and the Genius settled down to give me the detailed instructions for operating the "Forbidden Whisper."

After lights out I felt like a fugitive as I climbed out of my bunk and put on my coat and, having secured the door, began a routine which I was to follow successfully throughout the time I operated the set. First, I filled the stove with the night's allocation of fuel and then opened the window. Next, I went to the farthest end of the room, where I squeezed myself into the small gap between the locker and the end of the two-tier bunk. With my right foot underneath the bottom of the double locker, I lifted and swivelled it on the back far leg, towards me. This left me just enough space to put my left arm behind the locker and feel for the set. Having made contact, I lifted it carefully and very slowly until it was clear, then brought it towards me as I replaced the locker legs gently to the ground. I always left the locker in that position to assist in a quick replacement should there be a scare.

With infinite care I then carried our treasure to the table (I tremble to think what would have happened had I dropped it and broken it!). With it safely on the table I lifted the earphones, removed the bulb from my electric light and plugged in ready to switch on. After that I had to drape the aerial round the room. Later, after trying several methods of putting up the aerial to get the best reception, I found that the best results came when I used a short, direct aerial dropped out of the window, which worked far better than any of the inside aerial systems I could devise, though on mid-winter nights, only an Eskimo could have withstood the cold.

On this first night, I tried taking the aerial the whole distance around the room, hooking it up wherever possible. This done and now ready to switch on, with a sensation of incredible tension I fitted the 'phones over my ears.

As soon as I had thrown the switch, my ears were filled with noises. At least the set worked! With a concentration, to break which would have required a direct hit, I listened to every single sound, trying to make something coherent out of them. But it seemed to me that every station in Europe was on the air that night except the B.B.C. I estimated that there were about 20-odd stations within my range and not one of them was using the English language. The greatest offender was Radio Munich, which came up in surging waves and swamped everything for minutes at a time. If it was not Radio Munich, it was oscillation or atmospherics. For five hours I carried out the Genius' instructions and marked the panel every time I heard a station. Gradually, a dial radiating from the control knob was formed. They were five desperate hours and when finally even the stations easily received had closed down, I dismantled my aerial and replaced the Whisper in its hiding-place, removed the tin-opener from the door and climbed into my bunk a truly disappointed man.

Early next morning the Genius arrived to hear the news, and was not very encouraging in his remarks about my efforts. He suggested that it would be worthwhile to visit me after lights out, but I considered that this would be too risky and was happily able to dissuade him from doing so. I would get a report for certain the next night, I promised him.

Though my friends in the camp office were disappointed with my failure, they were sympathetic. The feeling of frustration which I sensed keenly made me all the more determined to get something at my next attempt.

So when I settled down with the Whisper on the second night, instead of draping the aerial around the room, I lowered it for about six feet out of the window. This seemed at once to give me better reception. Unfortunately, having found a way of avoiding Radio Munich, I got jammed up with Radio Breslau. But soon I began to get the hang of it. The slightest movement of the knob, even an imperceptible fraction of a millimetre, seemed to cover a wide range of stations. Little by little I became more selective, but I still could not make contact with an English speaking station.

As time went by, I began to get really desperate. The thought passed through my mind that I would have to concoct my own news bulletin because I just would not be able to confess a second failure. By midnight I was frantic, and decided to try every station I had recorded once more in the hope of picking up even a few words of English. With great care, I passed from one station to another, and as I did so, to my incredulous joy, I heard English being spoken. It was clearly news and I hoped it was the B.B.C.; but in trying to bring it up more clearly, I lost contact with it, and did not find it again before the air eventually went completely silent. However, I now knew that it was possible to get an English-speaking station and that was a step on the road to success.

Next morning I replied to the inevitable question: " Did you get anything? " with " The B.B.C." But when I had to explain that I had lost it almost as soon as I had found it, my stock, which had momentarily soared, dropped again to zero.

The Genius now refused to be put off coming over and taking a hand. As I was against his doing so after lights out, we compromised and arranged that he should visit me after evening roll-call. Fortunately that went off uneventfully and was soon over. I already had the set out and ready to work when he arrived and after securing the door, he went to work and began to make notes straight away. As time was short, he explained that I should get good results between this and that point on the dial, and informed me that as this was to be my last chance, I had better make the most of it.

Left on my own again, I faithfully followed instructions and at 10.30 was rewarded by identifying Radio Bari (which, by this time, was in Allied hands) and a quarter of an hour later I was crowned with success. Up came the 10.45 p.m. Overseas News Bulletin from the B.B.C. and I just cannot describe my feelings as I realised that all our efforts of the past weeks had not been in vain.

I decided that for safety I would build my report from the news given by Bari and the Overseas News; with the aid of carbon from the camp office, I made two copies. The news came in loud and clear and as fast as possible I made notes which I would be able to elaborate at my leisure when it was all over. I finished my report at about 10 minutes to midnight and thought that I would make just one more attempt to get the elusive B.B.C. Home Service Midnight News, but I had no great hopes. I nearly had a heart attack, therefore, when I heard the sound of Big Ben for the first time since I came to Germany.

I had only a three-watt bulb by which to work. The necessity of having the window open, which, in turn, meant having the black-out removed, made it impossible for me to use a stronger light. Working in this dimness as I had been doing for three nights now, was already beginning to strain my eyesight, and I decided that I could not go on like this. At a possibly slightly increased risk, having put the Whisper back into its hiding place, I closed the window, put up the black-out and fixed a blanket round the electric light into a structure closely resembling a wigwam, with a gap just big enough to take my head and shoulders. Once I was inside this contraption the ventilation became nil and I must have breathed the air in it many times over. But at least I could see.

First thing in the morning the Genius gave me a very severe ticking off for using too much volume. When I asked him how he knew, he told me that after leaving me the previous night, he had passed through the canteen while the set was giving forth music. Apparently the interference on that set was so loud that it frightened him to the extent of making his hair stand on end, but he believed it would have been too risky to come back to my room to tell me. I certainly used greater care after that.

The report I had managed to produce was well received and I had the feeling of satisfaction at being able to do something useful again. Since it was now possible to produce "the goods," it was decided that a camp news service should be started as soon as possible. Two men, Jock Davies and Wynne Sayer, would visit the rooms each evening and read the latest report.

The next evening I was once again successful and had completed a full report by 2 a.m. But next morning I overslept and was caught in bed and threatened with the fatigues which the Germans meted out to "long sleepers."

Soon the news service was in full swing. At first I produced two copies and then a third one to send over to the American side. The service came in for some distrust at the beginning because we could not let many know of the Whisper's existence. However, its value soon became apparent when it became a regular feature of camp life. I made no attempt to elaborate the news as I received it, and made every effort to make my report a faithful account of what I had heard.

When I had made the reports I neatly folded the sheets and hid them in the pillow-case on which I was sleeping. Before 6 a.m. the Shadow, Stan Keigthley, would collect them, return to his room with them, and before morning parade they would be safely in the hands of the news-readers, who were in honour bound to keep the contents secret until they made their evening rounds in the rooms. This method worked quite well until I could no longer put up with the rough handling I received from the Shadow when he came to collect the reports. He had a habit of lifting the pillow and tipping me against the wall, treatment which I did not appreciate after only four hours' sleep. So I undertook to making the delivery myself before I went to bed. Should I be discovered by some prowling German as I did so, I could always make a call of nature the excuse for being out of my room in the middle of the night, as the lavatories were on the Shadow's floor.

This worked out very satisfactorily until one very dark night I fell down the iron staircase and landed in a heap at the bottom. I hurt myself pretty badly and only just managed to reach my room and crawl into bed—with the news-sheets still in my possession—before passing out. Early next morning the Shadow looked in and demanded: "Why no newspapers?" When he had examined my bruises he promised that in future he would handle me with greater care, so we reverted to the former procedure.

At the beginning I was really scared stiff. Every now and then I would whip off the earphones and listen anxiously for any suspicious noise. On many occasions I switched off the set and sat for long minutes in the dark without moving a muscle, until I was satisfied that my fears were groundless. But there were two occasions which I shall always remember.

One lovely summer night I was confidently operating with the window open and the aerial dangling over the sill, when suddenly I froze in my chair as the German patrol below shouted: "Licht aus!" Not knowing quite what to do, I rapidly but as stealthily as I could pulled in the wire. I could not imagine how my little three-watt light could be visible from ground level 20 feet below, or by perimeter searchlight guards, but when the challenge was repeated followed by a threat to shoot and the perimeter searchlight seemed to focus on my window, I quickly gathered up the set and bits and pieces and hid them, hoping to beat the Germans to it. Then I clambered into bed and lay for some time petrified, expecting to hear the approach of German footsteps. When they did not come, I fell asleep, greatly relieved.

Next morning when I recounted my experiences in the camp office my somewhat abbreviated report was accepted without demur. Later, by way of the grapevine, I learned that the real culprit had been the man in the room below mine. He was a pro-German who, by virtue of the preferential treatment he received, was allowed to entertain his fellow sympathisers after lights out, up to a certain hour, which this evening he had exceeded. I was glad that I had not been the cause of the trouble.

The second occasion, which occurred at a much later stage of our operations, was, if possible, more alarming. I had just finished noting the B.B.C. midnight news and was about to replace the Whisper when several pairs of heavy boots stamped up the iron staircase leading directly to my door. It sounded like Hannibal's army of elephants, and I thought: This is IT.

Once again I sat petrified. From their loud conversation, I gathered that it was a Wehrmacht patrol bringing up to the cells one or more suspects or deserters. As my door was the first they came to, they tried several keys in the lock and attempted to open the door with each key. When they had exhausted their stock of keys, they began to bang on and kick at my door.

What my colour was while all this was going on I can only guess at. But I certainly offered up many prayers in rapid time and called on any and every mystic power to come to my aid before the tin-opener gave up the struggle and the door flew open, and I should be discovered sitting at the table with the Whisper before me — for I had no time to put it away.

After what seemed an eternity, they moved on to the next door, which they were able to open. There was a thud as the captive was flung in. This was repeated as they made their way along the cat-walk. Expecting a further assault on my door, I pushed everything against it that was easily movable. But they gave me no further trouble, and the sound of their receding footsteps, while bringing me relief, left me shaking. I wrote a hasty report and got into bed, just in case they should still be curious and return.

I followed a set routine nightly. When all the preliminaries were completed, I would tune into Radio Bari—which, after the Italian Armistice, was operated by the Allies — and make a quick note of the main points in the day's news. Then I would switch over to the B.B.C. Overseas broadcast to confirm and add to what I had just heard. After that I would take down the Forces Programme headlines at 11 p.m. and then put away the set from 11.15 to 11.45, when I would bring it out again for the B.B.C. midnight bulletin. Among the announcers for whose voice I would listen keenly were Joan Anderson and Jean Metcalf. While I awaited the midnight news, I would begin to write out my report in the wigwam, which I learned to erect at speed. The midnight headlines were very important to me, for very often my hastily written notes would resemble a Chinese puzzle when I began the sorting-out process. When I had put the Whisper away for the night, I would get down to producing my three copies. I would write down the headlines and then pick out what I considered to be the salient points, with which I filled in the space under each heading. If it happened to be a particularly vital broadcast — which was often — I had to go on to second sheets. I seldom got into bed until after 2 a.m. and the electric light I used must have contributed materially to the Third Reich's economic breakdown.

This routine I followed throughout the changing seasons. In the bitterly cold winter I operated with the help of the maximum allocation of fuel, but even so found it necessary to wear thick gloves with mittens over them, three pairs of socks, pyjamas under thick trousers, two jerseys, a balaclava helmet over my earphones, and a thick scarf to keep out any draught. And still my fingers and feet would become numb, for the job did not allow me to move at all, and I had the window open whenever I could bear it, because reception seemed to be so very much better with an outside aerial. Spring was pleasanter, and in the summer it would be so hot, even in the middle of the night, that for comfort I often worked in the " altogether." (Had I been found by a German guard in this condition, I should have found myself faced with additional problems, no doubt!). In autumn, conditions varied considerably.

At a rough assessment, I spent some 1200 hours listening to the Forbidden Whisper and writing bulletins. So attached to it did I become, that I found it impossible to part with it when the time came for us to leave Germany, and it became part of my personal luggage, and arrived safely in Guernsey. It is now in the Island Museum, but I had it for a time in my office and I often threw it a reminiscent glance. It occurs to me that many men have cause to thank that little set for their present mental health, for I am convinced that the camp news played a vital part in helping us to retain our sanity.

I do not think that anyone who has not had to rely on rumour and the moods and attitudes of camp guards for an idea of the progress of a war can possibly imagine how upsetting such a state can be. The wildest suggestions become current; wishful thinking often produces a rosier outlook than actual conditions justify; and then, if the truth should become known, or if theories do not work out in practice, the consequent mental depression can become well-nigh insupportable. Mind you, in the later stages of the War, and particularly after Stalingrad, it became comparatively easy to know that things were going badly for the Germans merely from the depression into which they progressively sank deeper and deeper. But it was nothing compared with being told exactly what was going on by a source which we knew to be 100 per cent reliable — the B.B.C.

Even so, this reliable news could, in its turn, be bad for the nerves. Though the rapid advance of the Russian armies under "Kanny" Koniev and "Jolly" Zhukov, which I was able to plot fairly accurately on a map "won" for us from the Camp Censor's office by a cleaner, cheered us up on the one hand, such events as the German break-through in the Ardennes, which made us wonder if our elation at the D-Day landings had not been premature, the long Russian pause before crossing the Vistula to capture Warsaw within 24 hours, the political implications of which we could not understand; the death of President Roosevelt — all these things cast the camp into a mood of the deepest despondency. Often, when I had reported the details of the Allied reverses, as officially stated in the news, I would wonder whether I was really doing the right thing in disseminating such news among our fellow internees.

But this was only a passing thought and, as I have said, the Forbidden Whisper did more for us than we have ever realised.

Chapter X

MACABRE ASSIGNMENT

IT IS NOW NECESSARY FOR ME to go back on my tracks a little. Probably one of the most dastardly crimes in World War II was the mass murder committed in the Forest of Katyn, about 14 miles from Smolensk, in Russia. The whole world was shocked when the full extent of the massacre was revealed.

The Germans were the first to give the news to the world. At the time they made their disclosure they were in occupation of the area in which the mass graves were situated, and they spared nothing to build up a case by what they called scientific research and documentation methods. Following the German announcements there came a long series of accusations and counter-accusations between them and the Russians. It is not my intention to take sides here, and I leave the reader to make his own decision when he has made his study of the material which I believe is available in the form of several books.

The news reached us in Laufen via the German radio and newspapers. It was at once obvious that something of world-wide import had been uncovered, and to us, prisoners of the Third Reich, who knew full well the depths that German brutality had plunged in the concentration camps of Belsen and Dachau and the rest, it seemed quite probable that this was a gigantic attempt to deceive the world.

There were a few in our camp, I believe, who realised how much importance the German High Command and the Propaganda Ministry attached to the matter. I did realise it in some degree, for I was told about it, in my official capacity as Camp Senior by the German Camp Captain, who stressed that it was a Russian atrocity and ought to give us British second thoughts about our allies. In fact, the

Germans hoped their revelations would be accepted by the West and cause a split with the Russians.

In view of what follows, I must put before my readers my personal interpretation and assessment of the responsibilities of a Camp Senior. Though we were civilian internees — which by any standard does not carry a very high status — we were British. As such I felt that we had received a certain degree of respect from the Germans, and that in return we must do everything possible to increase their respect for us, without actually becoming pro-German. This is only one point of view, I know, but I believed then, and still believe, that it was as valid as others, provided great care was taken not to play the Germans' game when it ran contrary to self-respect and patriotism.

One morning early in May, 1943, before the camp was fully astir, an urgent message was brought to the camp office demanding the immediate attendance of the Camp Senior before the German Camp Commandant. I reported without delay, and through the German Camp Captain, as interpreter, I gathered that an order had been received from the High Command under which British and American officers were to be "invited" to visit the mass graves at Katyn. Two responsible civilian internees were also to be included in the party.

As I saw it, though it was not a definite order that was given to me, it amounted to this: half an hour before morning parade I was to furnish the names of two internees who were willing to go to Katyn at the "invitation" of the German Propaganda Ministry. These two internees would be required to give an undertaking to render an account of their reactions and findings after the visit, possibly over the German radio, write articles for the German newspapers and visit prisoner of war camps to lecture about the scene. (The last would have been the hardest part of the undertaking to fulfil, for anyone can imagine the kind of reception which would have been given to any British national, especially a civilian internee, engaged on such a mission).

Immediately I understood what was wanted I refused to meet their request or co-operate with them in any way. I was then told that if I persisted in this attitude, volunteers from British internees would be called for on the morning parade, and from these men the Germans would make their own selection. I was then dismissed, and returned to the camp office.

I was very disturbed at this threat. I knew full well that with the assorted bunch we had in camp, the Germans would get enough volunteers to fill a plane, and that with the range of choice then available to them, they could easily pick out the man who would be prepared to jettison his British loyalty for the odd Reichmarks, schnapps and frauleins that would be thrown in.

Back at the camp office, I summoned a meeting of the Advisory Council members before they had had time to settle down to breakfast, and told them what had happened. I also told them what I thought would happen if we left it to the Germans to call for volunteers, and what might be the repercussions from the camp diehards if it became known that we " elders of the camp " had selected two men to go to Russia at the bidding of Goebbels' organisation. It seemed obvious to me that we must choose between the men willing to go and who were prepared to take the consequences of refusal to co-operate with the Germans after the visit to Katyn, though these consequences might make for a shortening of life.

It came as no surprise to me when Wynne Sayer, one member of the council, suggested that as I had so much to say about the project it would be a good idea if I went myself. I said I was quite willing to do this, which took him and, I believe, the others, back a bit. But he had a really nasty shock when he was proposed, seconded and elected to be the other member of the party; but he recovered his equilibrium pretty well and said he would be pleased to be associated with me in the venture.

Looking back on this meeting after a lapse of 13 years, and from the happy position of being wise after the event, I recall very clearly that it seemed to me that we were about to say farewell to our friends in Laufen for ever. We had no idea what might lie in store for us, nor what might be the outcome when we refused to do the Germans' bidding when the moment arrived.

My only request from the Advisory Council was that they should provide us with a document signed by all members, stating that the two men selected were volunteering to undertake the journey in the belief that they were

116

acting in the best interests of their country and of the camp. This document was to be used on our behalf only if we failed to stand by our undertaking not to help the Germans should they put us under super-human pressure. Incidentally, this authorization, agreed with one exception, David Savage, was lost after a Gestapo search of the camp.

At the appointed time I reported to the Camp Commandant and offered the names of our selected volunteers. If they were surprised that I was one of them, they said nothing, and I returned to the camp to await further developments. The Advisory Council had been sworn to secrecy, which they respected completely, and the camp, unaware of what was going on, remained calm except for the usual moans and groans about food, bed-bugs, snoring, etc.

Not knowing when I would be called upon, and provided the Propaganda Ministry accepted my name, I made all preparations and arrangements for a prolonged absence from Laufen at best, or at worst, my non-return.

The odd few shillings I had left in Guernsey I bequeathed to my wife, in a properly attested will, and handed the document for safe keeping to Len Collins, my best friend, and secretary to the Camp Senior. As usual, ribald suggestions were made about how I should dispose of my spare underpants and other personal belongings, and it was agreed that they should be left untouched for four weeks, after which lots should be drawn. There was a sizeable sum of money due to me from members of our bridge school, which we had operated on a credit system, but as payment was due in Camp Marks, I told them to paper the walls with them, metaphorically speaking, as and when they became available.

Late one evening about a week after we had taken our decision, I was sent for by the Camp Captain, who told me that an order had just arrived demanding that I should report to Berlin. I must be ready to leave at 4 a.m. the following morning. I questioned the order, as two internees had originally been required, but he told me that I was to be the one and only civilian in the party, which was not at all to my liking. But there was nothing I could do about it.

Until my departure next morning there was no rest in our office - cum - bed-sitting-room - cum-dining-room-cum-complaints-bureau. Great care was taken to use up all my tea ration, and the tea-pot, a converted Klim tin, was continuously in use throughout the night. The tea-drinking was accompanied with conversation which ranged over a wide selection of general topics and my trip in particular. They hoped it would keep fine for me, and wondered if, now that I was out on my Jack Jones, I would like to change my mind. Quite frankly, I was having second thoughts and although I have never been in that dreadful position, I imagine I felt like a man awaiting execution at dawn.

It seems very silly, looking back on it now, but when, just before 4 a.m., the door opened and a beckoning figure said "Komm," our emotions got a bit twisted and we had to make our parting snappy, otherwise it would have been a liquid one. Before the camp was astir I had left the Schloss, with my destination still secret from all but the Advisory Council and Camp Office. In the German office I was handed over to an unarmed soldier who spoke no English. At least, I told myself, I should have a quiet journey to Berlin. My escort, I believe, had been badly bashed about on the Eastern front, and for this reason was unable to march at the normal pace.

The first leg of our journey from Laufen to Freilasing, as I had feared, did not go according to schedule, but as it was very early on a fine May morning, and I was experiencing a false sensation of being at liberty, I did not mind. As we waited on the station for the train, there were very few people about, but at least there was no barbed wire. From the platform I could clearly see the Schloss, and I could not help looking for signs of life at the office window. But there was none. However, a coal fatigue party arrived shortly before the train came in and in answer to their questions I told them that I had been called in to advise the Führer on the future conduct of the War.

My guard was young and seemed to find his job greatly to his liking. He smoked my cigarettes with apparent enjoyment. Arriving at Freilasing, we had to wait three hours for a train to Munich, and as he seemed willing to make the journey as pleasant as possible, we went for a walk in the town, during which he revealed that he had some money for me which had been taken from my camp account and converted into Reichmarks.

At Munich, he reported to the military authorities and when the formalities were completed, he informed me that we had an 11-hour wait. Although my German was unintelligible, it was better than his English, so we agreed that it should be the means of communication between us. After a visit to a cinema reserved for the Wehrmacht, and to a museum and a café, we returned to the station, where we slept the time away on a bench. The place was packed with troops, and we had the usual air-raid warning, though nothing happened.

When I had first been told, 11 hours seemed a long time to wait for a train, but as the surrounding company was strange, my interest was held for some time. Then I thought for a time of my companions back in Laufen. Were they also thinking of me? Then I dozed a little, and so the time passed.

At long last, our train pulled into the station and before those wishing to alight had a chance to do so, a surge reminiscent of the opening day of the winter sales, only more so, began. My guard pushed and shoved me forward in the general direction of the train. There was no standing on ceremony, nor room to give proof of my natural instinct to make way for members of the opposite sex. Still our progress did not meet with the approval of my escort, and he issued a long statement, not a word of which I could understand. However, by a simple process of removing all obstacles that lay in our path, we eventually boarded the train.

As I was a prisoner, my comfort counted for nothing, and I was allotted a perch half in and half out on the platform at the rear of the carriage. Owing to the crush, I stayed there the whole of the 10-hour journey to Berlin.

It was just after midnight when we left Munich, so the first part of the journey was extremely cold. The crush of human bodies, however, helped to make it not quite as bad as it might otherwise have been; but as it was quite impossible to move my feet, they soon became solid blocks of ice, or at least they felt like it.

At every other stop, it seemed to me, the train was searched, and from what I saw I did not think that anyone hoping to travel on it illegally would have much chance of success. Apart from this, and a few vague general impressions, mostly of my discomfort, I remember little about that part of the journey. During the hours of darkness we seemed to be travelling through mountainous country. Whenever the train halted we had to bunch up even tighter to make way for new arrivals, until finally our condition was such that our very survival was imperilled.

When daylight came I was able to pass the time in a more entertaining way. By taking the opportunity of a halt to turn myself about, I was able to face outwards towards the country, instead of inwards, when my view was restricted to the nape of the neck of the man in front of me. I lost a certain amount of space by this manoeuvre, and had to abandon any thought of jumping the train as I knew that in the process I should lose my boots and my trousers, which already hardly seemed to belong to me at all.

The train ran towards the north-east, and so the country seemed to flatten out. As it was strange to me, and because I was convinced that I should not come back this way, I had a good look round.

We arrived in Berlin in the middle of the morning. On leaving the station, we took a short walk, then crossed a busy bridge which had guards posted at either end and seemed to span a canal. We turned right, and within half a mile reached our destination.

Chapter XI

PROPAGANDA IN SMOLENSK

THE REST OF THE PARTY were already in Berlin when I arrived. They were all servicemen and included English and American officers and N.C.O.s.

Perhaps they had good reasons for their cool reception of me. I had not expected to be met exactly with open arms. After all, I was only a civilian internee, and civilian internees have never been placed high in the social scale at any time, I suppose due to the fact that a very mixed bag always ranges under their banner. Nevertheless, I was not prepared for their welcome, which had in it a breath of the Arctic wastes.

Perhaps I made a mistake in volunteering the information that I had come of my own free will. I did not feel in a position to question how these English and American officers and N.C.O.s came to be here. When at last I was able to ask the C.O. of the party for his advice, and told him that I would welcome any orders he would like to give me, he informed me quite definitely and, without doubt, correctly, that he would not accept any responsibility for me; nor would he give me any orders or advice beyond telling me that all the servicemen were refusing to go to Russia. Though I was out on my own, I would be well advised to follow a similar course, and he reminded me that I should be liable under the Defence of the Realm Act— the Treachery Act was not put in the Statute Book until 1945—if I did anything contrary to my duty as a British national.

By dressing in my best suit, with a collar and tie, I had hoped to give the impression that I was a respectable British citizen, rather than a scruffy internee. Possibly I looked too smart, and it may have been that they believed me to be a collaborator.

At all events, I felt very uncomfortable and was greatly disappointed to sense that I was suspect. However, the two N.C.O.s whose room I shared did not send me to Coventry.

I cannot swear to my memory being 100 per cent correct, but I am pretty sure that we were housed in a tall building near a canal, and not far from a bridge which seemed to carry the main road to one of Berlin's great railway termini. This was the view from the front windows. From the windows of my room, which was on the top floor rear of the building, all that could be seen was chimney pots and roof tops, and what we believed to be the dome of the burnt-out Reichstag building in the distance. The customary air-raid warning sounded shortly after I arrived, but as Allied heavy bombing had not yet become a regular feature of Berlin's life, nothing seemed to happen.

I certainly did not look forward to the idea of appearing before the German authorities and telling them that having come all this way I had changed my mind and please could I go home (meaning back to Laufen) and I pondered deeply what I should do. When eventually the time came for the interview, I was ushered into a large room, the walls of which were lined with maps. At a long table sat a number of very important looking individuals, with the one who seemed to be the big chief at the end and directly facing me. In the few brief seconds which passed before he spoke to me, the world-famous picture of Cavalier and Roundhead days entitled: " When did you last see your father? " flashed through my mind.

I was asked my name and other unimportant details, and then questioned about why I had volunteered to go to Russia. I agreed that I had volunteered and then, with a rush of words and as boldly as I could, I said that I had now changed my mind, pointing out that I had only just realised that as I was a British subject I was liable to the penalties provided by the Defence of the Realm Act if I did anything which aided my country's enemies. Before I had really finished I was given my answer, which was to the effect that, having been brought to Berlin, I was going to finish the journey whether I liked it or not. They went into a brief huddle, not one word of which I understood, and I was told to return to my room.

When I rejoined the others, naturally they were anxious to know what I had said. I told them and they agreed that I had at least done the correct thing and I thought the ice began to thaw a little. I felt fairly pleased with myself; so far I had not compromised my British nationality.

Later in the day the C.O. called us all to a conference and informed us that in spite of the fact that the Germans had received 100 per cent refusal to co-operate any further, they had decided that we should all go to Katyn. We should be sent under armed guard; that is, we should go as prisoners and not of our own free will. I gathered that this had been expected by the party. The C.O. further emphasized that we must continue in our resolve not to co-operate either on the journey or afterwards, when the trip was over. I cannot say what a relief it was to be included now in the general policy, and for the first time since I had arrived in Berlin I lost the sensation of being the odd man out.

After the conference we went back to our rooms. The N.C.O.s and I had as an attendant a Russian P.O.W. from Leningrad who spoke a little English. Apparently he had been a medical student before being captured while fighting somewhere on the Baltic coast. He was not very communicative but elected to tell us that before we left Berlin we were to be taken on a tour of the city. As usual, I spoke out of turn, saying that it was very nice of our hosts to entertain us in this way, and I was warned not to fall for any of this smooth treatment, which was merely an attempt to soften us up and make us more co-operative.

The Russian was quite right. Early in the afternoon a bus arrived to take us to see the sights of the city. It was a gas-driven bus—a type then being used extensively throughout Germany—and had attached to the rear of it a contraption not unlike Heath Robinson's perpetual motion gadget.

We were ushered into it and set out on tour. The parts of the city we were shown, which I have since tried to identify on a map but failed, were not extensively damaged by bombs, which was not surprising since, as I have already pointed out, the Allied bombing offensive had not yet gathered momentum. Several places we passed bore familiar names, but the incident which stands out most in my memory of the afternoon was the bus passing out on us as we came to the bottom of a steep hill. I do not think the

Germans were particularly pleased about this as they had been lauding the superior qualities of the gas-driven bus over the petrol-driven. However, after waiting for some time we were presented with three alternatives which seemed to amount to this; first, we could stay in the bus for the duration of the war; second, we could get out and push it; third, we could walk to the top of the hill and hope that "Wheezy-Anna" would be able to make it, empty. We all chose the third and walked up the hill while the bus progressed in fits and starts after us.

Either by original intent or by a rearrangement of the itinerary, the rest of the tour was either downhill or on level ground, and after collecting us from, I believe, the Opera House, we returned to our quarters to spend a night disturbed by air-raid warnings. The following morning the treatment continued. An early morning walk was arranged for those who wished, along the road outside the building and on our return we were given breakfast and told to get ready to leave for the airport. By this time I was feeling much more confident. Though I could not help reflecting on the great difference between the status of the prisoner of war and of the civilian internee, at least I felt "so far so good . . ."

We took off from Tempelhof Airport, east-bound, at about nine o'clock, and made our first stop at Breslau, where the Junkers troop carrier in which we were being conveyed stopped to refuel. From there, having passed within sight, but to the south of Warsaw, we next touched down at a small town which I believed was called Sokowpol and which, from its activity, I thought must be a maintenance depot for the Luftwaffe in the east. Here we stopped for lunch, which was served with all the trimmings, and I realised that the V.I.P. treatment was being stepped up.

Reboarding the plane and heading east, between bouts of violent air-sickness, I was able to note that we were passing over the ancient frontier fortress town of Minsk. These bouts of sickness had started very shortly after we had left Berlin; I think that being scared stiff was the cause of the trouble.

After Minsk, the huge area of Russia stretched out before us. From the air it seemed that the land was quite flat, and for the whole of the four hours which this leg of the journey took, we flew at a very low altitude, going even lower as we neared Smolensk. When I asked the reason for this I was told that there were Russian fighter planes in the vicinity, information which, combined with the air-sickness, made me long for Laufen more than ever.

In May, 1943, the German lines of communication were stretched, like elastic, almost to breaking point. Their eastward drive had come to a full-stop east of Smolensk, about 200 miles west of their objective, Moscow. To the novice in warfare, or to any average civilian internee, for that matter, it appeared that the Russian scorched earth policy was adding greatly to the German difficulties and taking heavy toll of their resources, since this policy meant that the Russian population in the huge areas under German control were almost without food or shelter. Such a situation makes even the most docile of men desperate, particularly if he has a family. To attempt to feed the enemy if only on a scale which would make him more amenable, meant a terrific burden on the already fast emptying larders of the Third Reich, for even the conquered countries of the West had by now been bled white of food. All supplies travelling either by road or rail over great distances were subjected to continual and increasing interference from Russian partisan guerilla bands who, with their intimate knowledge of the terrain, could roam at will. These guerillas succeeded not only in seizing or destroying German supplies but kept a large number of Germans out of the front line in an attempt to control them, and to protect the convoys.

The historic city of Smolensk was at this time the forward base of the German armies advancing on Moscow, and forces and supplies were being steadily built up there to meet the threat of the Russian counter-offensive which must surely come. Again, purely from my personal observations in the city—and we were shown only what the Germans wanted us to see—I formed the opinion that the Germans already realised that they would get no further east. It was not just a question of stopping to get their breath; they had, in fact, shot their bolts.

At Smolensk Airport we were met by the official reception committee and driven off in staff cars. It was obvious that the greeting was meant to assure us that we were with friends among the enemy, and again it occurred to me that the Germans were attaching great importance to our visit to the Katyn graves and were hoping that they would be able to derive good propaganda capital from it.

To the untravelled civilian who had recently been cooped up in a camp behind wire, this was a real sight-seeing tour and I intended to make the best of it, in case it should turn out to be the last one I should ever have. So from the beginning I was all ears and eyes.

As I already knew, Smolensk had suffered from a much earlier invader. In 1812 the inhabitants, fleeing to Moscow before the advance of Napoleon's armies, had also employed the scorched earth policy and left the city in flames, and there is no doubt that the scorching of Smolensk had contributed to his failure to take Moscow, and to his ultimate defeat in that campaign. We were shown the museum containing historic relics and the gate through which Napoleon had begun his retreat back to France, and the garden in which, it was claimed, the Emperor reached the vital decision to cut his losses and go home [See plate 7].

Time plays tricks with the memory, but from what I can recall the city stands principally on two hills, and through the valley which they form the Dnieper runs, gathering itself thereafter until it finally becomes one of Russia's mightiest rivers. It waters the vast wheat-bearing plains of the Ukraine and supplies great quantities of hydro-electric power through one of the world's greatest dams at Dniepropetrovsk, before it empties itself into the Black Sea. At Smolensk it is a graceful river, with the railway line to the west lying in its valley on its right bank. At the time of our visit this railway was the German lifeline, and armoured trains were giving protection to the convoys both in and out of the city.

It had taken us eight hours to reach Smolensk from Berlin, and we were at once taken to staff quarters and given a meal. When this was over an all-male entertainment was staged to put us in a receptive mood, and then we went to bed with guards posted at our doors to see that we did not try to see the sights unescorted.

The next morning, as the C.O. had predicted, the treatment was continued. The full extent of the scorched earth policy was seen as we drove out of the town to the newly-built German hospital. I was appalled by the wanton destruction. Scarcely a building had escaped.

Naturally we had to accept the facts given to us by the Germans, and what they told us was incredible. Over 30,000 people had stayed behind after the city had been burned and there were only 25 buildings fit for habitation. From what I saw, I thought that for once the Germans were not exaggerating. There was not a pane of glass to be seen in any of the gaping windows along our route and, indeed, all that seemed to remain were just hollow shells. Even though we were being taken by a route selected by the Germans for the greatest effect, it really made me wonder what the future of mankind would be when there were people living prepared to destroy so ruthlessly their own cities, let alone the cities of their enemies.

The people who had remained behind were living in pitiful conditions, mostly in cellars with anything they could salvage to shelter them. This was May and the weather was beautiful, but what their conditions had been like in the previous winter and would be like in the winter ahead—for although the Germans were just beginning to rebuild they would not be able to touch the fringe of the problem by October, when the snows and below zero temperatures come —made the imagination boggle. In fact, I often thought of the people of Smolensk when I was working the Forbidden Whisper under several layers of clothing and, at worst, had a bed to go to. It was clearly obvious that 30,000 people could not live here and when someone said so, we were told that large numbers were living outside the city in shanty towns where their food and sanitation were controlled by the Germans, who also provided hospital treatment for the worst cases. We were not taken to see one of the " towns," however.

Over and over again, our escorts assured us that their advancing armies had been responsible for none of the destruction, but that the Russians had themselves done all this. Although much of the destruction had been caused by fire, it seemed to me that the city had been methodically destroyed by an army of men dismantling and removing everything of any possible use to a future occupier, and what they could not remove they burned or smashed.

The city in peace was dominated by the Russian Orthodox Cathedral, built on the highest point of one of the hills It still dominated this scene of utter destruction for alone of all the buildings of Smolensk, it seemed unharmed. Why it was left untouched, I cannot think, for long before the Germans came it had ceased to be a place for Christian worship. Inside, it was not defaced and the high altar and vestments were well kept, though they were told it had been used as a museum to ridicule religion. It had been the Germans, we were assured, who had returned it to the people for use as a House of God, as it had been in former times, and crowds had come to worship there.

When we visited this cathedral a mass was being celebrated before quite a large congregation. I think what impressed me most about it were the 60 or more steps which led up to the main entrance. These steps were so worn that it was evident that many thousands of the faithful had come to this place since it had been built, though some of it had doubtless been the result of the treading of children's feet, brought here so they might have impressed upon them that all religions were only fit to be laughed at and spat upon. We were then taken into the south-west area of the city and out on to the main Smolensk-Kiev road, which, due to the recent heavy rain and continuous flow of traffic, had been reduced to a sea of mud. It was, in fact, little better than a cart track full of pot-holes and deep ruts.

For this drive field transport of the jeep type was provided for us. We passed many parties of refugees, who clogged up the road as they wandered aimlessly in the vain hope of finding shelter in that land of utter desolation. Refugees present a major problem to an army either advancing or retreating, and from what I saw of the problem here —at a time which the Germans claimed was more or less normal—it must have been an extraordinary one.

After some miles we turned off the main road into a secondary road which, by our standards, was not a road at all. The object of this part of our tour was to impress on us the way in which a race of " cultured " conquerors could raise the masses of the people to a standard of existence which their own countrymen could never hope to give them. Somehow the example chosen to impress us failed in its object.

The housing conditions of the Russian peasant have for centuries been among the most squalid of all human habitations in the world, and one wonders what joy they can get out of living. The normal peasant dwelling is a dark, stinking, thatched hut, comprising one room for living, cooking and sleeping. A hole in the roof serves to let out the smoke from the fire of peat or wood; the door, and perhaps one window, let in light and air.

The greater part of the living-room is taken up by a large flat-topped oven on which, in winter, the whole family sleeps, huddled together for extra heat. The proudest possessions of the peasant family are the livestock, kept in and around the house. At night all the animals share the living-room with the family, and often they and human beings lie close together in their search for warmth in the 40 or 50 degrees of frost which clamps down on them for two or three months of the year. Often the villages are attacked by packs of hungry wolves at this time. Almost the only activity in the worst winter months is hunting for food—game, fowl and fish. These people have no use for money. For any work they do they are paid in kind.

On this May day the sea of mud through which we floundered was already beginning to harden a little. As the summer months approached, months which would be as hot as the winter months were cold, it would gradually be baked to the hardness of steel. Then violent dust storms would add to the misery of the people.

When one of us remarked that the people seemed well fed, the escort replied that this was due to the sympathetic treatment which had been shown them by their conquerors. Soon, they boasted, they would raise the standard of all Russian peasants to that which they were now about to show us.

Presently we noticed a great improvement in the surface of the road and soon arrived at the show-piece. It was a model village, with good roads, small but compact one-storey houses, with good ventilation and sanitation—a new sewage farm was being developed to provide the latter—a village hall which combined the functions of school, cinema and lecture-hall. There was also a church, but the show-piece was the model farm equipped with every modern farming device. A large number of pigs were housed in solid styes, and the hygiene of the whole farm was of the highest standard.

The complete population of the village, it seemed, turned out to see the visitors and looked as if they had been dressed up for the occasion. Possibly they were used by now to being put on display.

The grandfather of the community, looking very much like Rasputin's uncle, was introduced, and made us an address of welcome which, though it was so much Russian to us, had obviously been well rehearsed. We were fully aware that this show had been put on entirely to impress us, nevertheless, one could not help feeling that if only the living conditions of all Russian peasants could be brought up to the standard of this model village, the masses of humanity living in this great wilderness would have some object in living, which did not seem to be the case at present.

Our visit completed, we returned to our quarters and were entertained to dinner—front-line type—by the officials of what I thought must be the propaganda unit, together with members of the investigating body at the Katyn Wood site. Everything, especially the attitude of the Germans, was strictly correct. A sufficient number of English-speaking men had been gathered together so that there could be general conversation in our own language.

During a pause in the meal and afterwards, we were entertained by a Cossack unit which was part of the White Russian contingent serving alongside the Germans, but under their own General. It was all typically Russian and consisted of songs and dances to the accompaniment of the balalaika. When this was finished, we were allowed to take exercise in the barrack square, and as we walked round in pairs, we naturally turned to the subject of our forthcoming visit to the mass graves, the main object of our being brought here. The C.O. gave us yet another reminder regarding our status and of the need for great care to be taken to avoid being trapped into making some incriminating statement which might afterwards be used for enemy propaganda.

So another day ended, during which it had become obvious that at least until our visit was over, we could expect highly favoured treatment. But I must confess that one of the thoughts uppermost in my mind was: What would happen when the time came for me to tell the Germans that they had really wasted their time, efforts, money and petrol? This thought, I believe, was most responsible for my broken night's sleep—or was my first experience of vodka partly to blame?

Chapter XII

THE FOREST OF KATYN

AS SOON AS WE HAD finished breakfast the next morning, we were taken by our armed escort to waiting staff cars. The road we took ran westwards out of Smolensk and was, in fact, the Smolensk-Vitebsk-Minsk highway. Since this road was tremendously important to the Germans, as it was their life-line for supplies coming from the West, I was not surprised to find it in an excellent state of repair. It runs roughly parallel with the railway and has long, straight stretches, which make it capable of taking heavy traffic at high speeds.

About 12 miles to the west of Smolensk we passed a small railway station which, we were told later, had played a vital rôle at the time of the drama of Katyn. A short way further on we crossed over the railway, drove on for another three miles or so, and eventually came to a halt before the heavily guarded entrance to a tree-lined drive leading into the forest. As we waited for the barricade to be moved, I became aware of a strange odour which I could not identify at once. Then, still in the cars, we drove up the gentle slope of the drive for about a quarter of a mile.

When the cars stopped, we were told that we had arrived at the site of one of the most terrible massacres in history. There was no need to tell us this since the strange smell, which had gained strength as we came up the drive, was now overpowering in its sickly, nauseating stench, and was now identifiable as the odour of rotting corpses, the terrible odour of death. I had never experienced it before and I hope that I shall never experience it again.

As we approached the huge grave, I noted that it was situated on high ground, and I recalled reading a report which referred to the area as " Goat Hill " and described the soil as being sandy clay in nature. Although we were well inside the actual forest, there were very few trees and

132

they were young and small and planted far apart. Although there were still patches of snow lying about and the ground seemed still to be frozen hard, it was such a beautiful day that it was not necessary to wear overcoats. I held a handkerchief over my mouth and nose but could not prevent the horrible stench from entering my lungs as it was blown into our faces by the light breeze. To those working on the site it must have been really unpleasant. Russian P.O.W.s and numbers of the local inhabitants were being used for the actual excavation work.

The Germans seemed pretty sure of themselves. We were told that any questions we cared to ask would be answered fully, and that a number of inspections had already been carried out by parties from neutral countries. A short distance outside the forest, and on the main highway, they had erected a large single-storeyed barrack hut to act as a museum for the large collection of documents, relics taken from the graves and any other evidence which added point to their case against the Russians [See plate 8].

The case, as presented to us and to any other investigating party was, of course, a purely one-sided interpretation. But it had been built up carefully by the best brains which Germany could provide for this sort of work and had about it, at least, the aura of authenticity. To support it they brought the evidence of the local Russian inhabitants which, however, though we were assured had been given voluntarily and eagerly, could have been forcibly extorted.

Even after seeing it all, the graves, the thousands of bodies, the museum, all the evidence, I still do not feel capable of giving an opinion as to who were the perpetrators of the horrors of Katyn. To believe the German version as it was presented to us would require shutting out of one's mind all knowledge of the atrocities committed by them— Belsen, Dachau, Mauthausen, the notorious concentration camps, and the terrible incident of the Ardeatine Caves, just outside Rome, when the Germans executed 350 Italians in batches of five before the eyes of those who were also to be killed.

The background history of the affair is easy to follow. It begins with the non-aggression pact signed by Ribbentrop and Molotov in the August of 1939, which cleared the way for the German attack on Poland without fear of Russian opposition. It goes on with the heroic but hopeless resistance of the gallant Polish armies and their final defeat by the combination of the German frontal attack and the Russian stab in the back.

According to the German version, the Poles captured by the Russians were taken to prison camps far inside Russia and kept there in shocking conditions until the early spring of 1940, when the camps were gradually disbanded. When this happened, the lower ranks among the prisoners were either returned to their own country or kept in Russia for forced labour. From this time, however, almost the entire officer cadre of the Polish army, numbering between 12,000 and 15,000 men, vanished without trace. The Germans claimed that evidence in their possession established proof that several thousands of Polish officers passed through Smolensk in May, 1940, from the general direction of the camps which were disbanding, but after passing through Smolensk they disappeared, so to speak, into thin air.

Despite diligent search in their own country and in spite of many appeals to the Russians from their friends and relatives, nothing could be learned of the fate of the vanished Polish officers. Then came the gruesome find, which, the Germans claimed, solved the mystery. It solved the mystery of the fate of the Polish officers, certainly, but it did not solve the mystery of who was responsible.

One of the main flaws in the German argument, to my way of thinking, was the fact that two years elapsed after they had taken this part of Russia (the Germans had occupied Smolensk within two months of the initial Hitler attack on Russia) before they made their discovery. I should have liked to ask the reason for this but I decided that it would be best to keep my mouth shut and just listen to what I was being told. That way, I could not be accused afterwards of doing anything which would help the enemy.

We were led to the edge of a mass grave, which was a great L-shaped pit. I estimated that it was about 80 yards long and 30 yards wide, with a depth varying to a maximum of 20 feet. This pit was on the highest part of Goat Hill and was therefore free from water, but it held a slimy, sticky substance which was from the decomposing bodies. Various reports I had read in Laufen had claimed that there were between 9,000 and 12,000 bodies in the graves. This great pit could certainly have held 5,000, for the bodies were packed eight deep in places. Besides the great pit, there were several smaller graves, all filled with bodies.

Several layers of bodies had already been removed from the pits. We were made to examine some of them and it was clear that they had been killed by a shot, fired at very close range, into the base of the skull; earth in the throats of some of the corpses indicated that they had still been breathing when flung into the pit. The sight filled me with horror. I just have not the words to describe either the scene or my feelings. It was a nightmare. How could it happen in this enlightened age that members of one race could commit such a terrible crime against their fellow men?

We were made to walk the full length of the grave. The sight of this packed mass of human bodies and the ghastly stench of death, almost made me pass out. Other members of our party were visibly affected by the terrible sight. But we had to go on. There was no way out, and as we tottered uncertainly the whole length of the grave walking between and on the piled stacks of bodies, our German guards kept up an endless drone about the horror of this Russian atrocity, which came strangely from the perpetrators of Ravensbruck and Auschwitz.

From the bonds which still tied the hands of the victims behind their backs, it seemed that they had offered some resistance, before being made to kneel on the edge of the pit for execution. I was surprised by the excellent state of preservation of much of the clothing covering the bodies and even more so by the paper evidence found on or near the corpses, for some of the writing was still easily legible. These facts did much to prevent me from being convinced. Against it, however, though even this could be argued either way, this particular part of the forest had been used for many years by the Russians as a burial ground for executed criminals. Their graves could be seen scattered about the vicinity of the site and they covered a wide area. Altogether, it was too difficult, I found, for any ordinary man to make up his mind one way or the other on the evidence put before us.

The drive by which we had approached the site continued on past the graveyard and ended near to a " dacha " or summer house, on the banks of the river Dneiper. This, we were told, had been used as a rest house for members of the Russian Secret Police. Apart from the fact that the surrounding area contained such grisly relics, it would have made an ideal place for a party in the spring or summer.

When at last we left this terrible place, we were taken to the museum and shown the relics already collected there. It seemed that no effort had been spared by the Germans to strengthen any weak link in their chain of evidence. But here again, I found it impossible fully to be convinced. The more one thought about it, the more one was brought to the conclusion that what was being done was rather more of a serious effort to cause a split between the Allies than from any moral considerations. At this time, the Germans must have known that their defeat at Stalingrad had placed them in a very difficult position, and that in the West the Allies were also preparing to launch the final attack on them. Anything they could do, therefore, to weaken the fighting friendship between the Western powers and Russia might be very much in their favour.

After the War it became clear that the Germans had withheld some of the evidence and exaggerated other parts of it as, for example, the number of corpses in the mass graves. The Nuremberg trials elicited the fact that there were only 4,000 corpses at Katyn instead of the 9,000 to 12,000 claimed by the Germans; also, the date was fixed as the autumn of 1941, when the Germans were in occupation of the territory. I doubt whether the mystery will ever definitely be cleared up.

When the time came for our party to leave for our return journey to Smolensk I must admit that it was a great relief to me to leave behind the awful smell of death and the sight of those thousands of mutilated bodies. As we went I turned over in my mind what I had seen and the effect it had had on me and I felt somehow stronger now to refuse to play the Germans' game, though the moment of saying so was not one to which I was looking forward with relish.

None of us spoke on our way back to the city for the simple reason that not one of us had the words to describe his feelings.

Chapter XIII

RETURN JOURNEY

AT THE SMOLENSK BARRACKS, the treatment meted out to us was even more calculated to soften us up than anything we had previously experienced. The climax was reached at the evening meal, for which the Germans had collected together, it seemed, every English-speaking German east of the Rhine, for each one of us had his own special companion. On the face of it, they were pleasant types, but had obviously been hand-picked for the job.

The man detailed to look after me claimed to have been born in North London, right on my own doorstep, in fact. I gathered that he was a staunch Arsenal supporter, and that his second choice was the Spurs. He was quite young and obviously very keen on making a good job of the task in hand. He was very clever, too, and I had to take continuous evasive action to keep off the subject of Katyn. I was lucky in being a keen sportsman and knowing something about both the teams he claimed to support. In this way I steered the conversation clear of any discussion of my future activities. I also tried, in a roundabout way, and I think I succeeded, to make it quite clear to him that as far as I was concerned there was nothing doing. I told him in so many words that I wanted to see both Arsenal and Spurs play again some day and so I had no intention of doing anything which might result in my getting my neck stretched after the War was over. Smiling, he assured me that I should not see any Friendly, League or Cup game for a very long time, as London was *kaput*.

When at last we were sent to our quarters, I felt happy at being over the first hurdle and my confidence increased, though not to such an extent that I no longer feared the final interview.

The following morning we left Smolensk by air and following closely the road and rail routes, we eventually touched down at the same airfields as on our outward journey. Lunch that day was well up to standard but I had to accept hearsay evidence on that, for the air journey was, if possible, worse than when we came out. This, and what lay before us in Berlin, caused me to be prostrated with airsickness. We ran into violent squalls and hail storms, which slowed us up considerably. By the time we had landed in Berlin I was more dead than alive. I longed only for bed, and when I reached it I fell into it and thought no more about tomorrow's " inquest ".

My confidence, which was beginning to wane slightly by the morning, received renewed strength when the C.O. re-primed me and I rehearsed my part to word perfection. It was merely a question of waiting for my turn now, and presently it came.

The moment I went into the room to face the " committee " my mind, fortunately, steadied. I was asked whether I had been to Russia and to Katyn, to which I answered " Yes " and then came the 64,000-dollar question: " What personal view had I been able to form? " Quite firmly I replied that I had not been able to form any conclusive opinion one way or the other, and immediately I sensed a cooling of their attitude towards me, which up to then had been quite friendly. I went on quickly to say that I was still of the same mind that I had been before I left Berlin and that I was not prepared to do anything which would jeopardise my standing as a British national. They took no more trouble over me then and dismissed me back to my room.

I must admit that I was very relieved. Looking back now, it seems that the anticipation of that meeting was worse than the reality. When the whole party had been interrogated individually and returned to their quarters, the C.O. called us together to discuss what might happen to us now. He thought we might be kept in Berlin for a time while a decision was made about what to do with us. We might be sent to camps different from those from which we had come. As we had all stuck to the same story, the Germans might deal with us as a unit, but I gathered that they did not think much of my chances as a civilian internee.

Returning to our own rooms for a meal, our Russian attendant informed us that the chief of the examining "committee" before whom we had just appeared was an Englishman, none other than William "Lord Haw-Haw" Joyce. This fact I cannot confirm, but at least it gave us something to talk about.

In the early evening I was ordered downstairs again. I went a little weak in the knees, being quite convinced that "this was IT." But when I arrived at the ground floor, I was told that I was to be sent back to Laufen, and that my escort would be coming for me soon.

I went back to the room to collect my few things together. Having taken the opportunity to wish the others good-bye and good luck, I was advised to keep constantly on my guard, and in fact, never to open my mouth about the journey nor what I had seen all the time I was in enemy hands. Other members of the party had not received any orders so I left them behind in Berlin. I understand, however, that after some days they were disbanded, some returning to their former camps, some to new ones.

The return journey to Laufen was possibly worse than the journey to Berlin. It took 12 hours to Munich and we were in darkness nearly all the time. I had a strange feeling of being nearly home when at last we reached Munich and, fortunately, we had to wait only two hours for the train to Freilasing. Here, however, we were held up. Laufen was served only by a sort of milk-train service and the trains were few and far between.

It never before occurred to me that the sight of Laufen could be so inviting, but when I looked at the Schloss in the distance it was just that. As I marched through the camp gates my thoughts may have been confused but I was conscious of one predominating feeling — I was HOME!

In the camp office scenes reminiscent of the return of the Prodigal were enacted. They told me that they had been able to wangle my rations in my absence, so we had high tea.

Without wishing to infer in any way that by going to Russia I did something no other Camp Senior would have done, I do nevertheless feel convinced that I did the right thing when I made my decision. Still, it is always easy to be wise after the event.

For a considerable time afterwards I was the object of suspicion by several of the internees. As the Germans were quick to realise this and applied a little subtle pressure of their own, it did not help me in my office of Camp Senior and the job had been bad enough before; but my many friends helped me by not asking me any questions and persuading others to behave likewise, and I appreciated their help very much.

It was certainly an experience, but one I could well have done without; and I was glad and relieved when it was all over.

Having once more settled down to internment, I had ample time to reflect fully on the events of the recent past; I concluded that the whole of the " conducted tour " had been carried out with a degree of propriety I had not anticipated and certainly not dared to hope for at the outset. The entire incident leaves me personally convinced that in the High Places in Nazi Germany doubts were already being raised about a final victory by force of arms. Therefore it was vital for them to find a " miracle " which would lessen the blow or split the powers ranged against them. So, in my opinion, did the Germans grasp at presenting Katyn to the world.

The whole venture must have proved a disappointment to the German Ministry of Propaganda. It seemed that they had hoped to secure support for their case from the visit of British and American prisoners. Without doubt they misjudged the situation when they tried to get assistance from enemy nationals.

Chapter XIV

LIBERATION

ON MY RETURN FROM KATYN, my position as Camp Senior became more and more difficult. The reason was that several regarded my action in going with suspicion. As I have already described, the situation came to a head when, trying to be wise, I suggested that we should cut down on our consumption of Red Cross parcels so that when the Allies began to put pressure on the enemy's communications and the parcels ceased to arrive, we should not starve. My visit to Russia had, I think, inspired the viewpoint.

If my resignation had not been more or less forced on me, I do not quite know what I should have done. As it was, the decision was made for me and I was relieved, in more ways than one.

Now that the administrative duties of the camp office no longer occupied my time I threw myself first into helping in the construction of the Forbidden Whisper and then, when it was built, operating it. Here again, I have to say that had it not been for the interest and activity which the wireless provided for me, I do not know what I should have done with my time.

After two years of camp life, we had settled down to a routine. There were, of course, the individual routines, all of which varied slightly, one from the other. But overall there was the general programme. We ate at such and such hours, we played games then and then, we went to roll call regularly, we had our bridge schools or our poker sessions from this o'clock to that o'clock.

Really the trouble was that though we were prisoners, held behind wire, deprived of our freedom, we were not actually physically uncomfortable. Red Cross food parcels arrived and were issued regularly—almost to the point of monotony—though in saying this, naturally, I do not wish to detract in any way from the great work of the Red Cross;

the Y.M.C.A. continued to supply our wants for both physical and mental relaxation. In fact, we had reached such a point that the grousers were very hard put to it to find anything to grouse about. To give us a feeling of security the Protecting Power—the Swiss—was in constant touch with us. Nevertheless, with all these comforts, our great enemy was boredom, and there are few things which more quickly undermine the morale than boredom. Several of the internees were entirely without internal resources with which to fill the many hours on their hands, and these people spent the greater part of the days, weeks and months on their beds, plunged in depths of despondency.

Those who had some resources, or realised what would happen to them if they had nothing to occupy their minds and hands, as the case might be, according to their temperament, made interests for themselves, even if it meant annoying their room mates, and these fared better than the others.

Classes in many subjects were now well organised and well attended, and those who wished had ample opportunity for increasing their learning.

The Camp Senior's office now took on the appearance of a municipal organisation and became deeply entangled in the tentacles of bureaucracy. There was an elaborate filing system, every document was produced in duplicate or triplicate. This may have kept some happy but to me it did not represent progress from the early days when every scrap of paper we could lay our hands on scarcely supplied essential needs. Where then we had written on both sides of the paper and filled in the margin as well, now there were wide, clean margins, and the paper was used on one side only. Despite all this we lacked one thing—freedom—and this was having a corrosive effect on the mental and physical health of the active and inactive alike. It was not as though we had been given definite sentences and could look forward to a date for our release from captivity. It was the factor of unknown duration that irritated us most.

One or two incidents stirred the camp out of its lethargy a little. Since the internal organisation was running so smoothly and the departmental staffs were in control of duties, some of the civilian internees who had formerly held officer rank and clung to their titles in retirement made a new claim for recognition of their status; this was supported by the new Camp Senior and they were excused from camp fatigues unless they wished to volunteer, thus completely reversing the policy of absolute equality of all civilian internees. I do not wish to give the impression that all those who had received a commission supported the demand. In fact, very many promptly volunteered for fatigues.

For a day or two the introduction of this measure was the chief topic of conversation in the camp. It is indicative, however, of the condition of mind into which we had fallen that it was accepted—when the initial irritation had worn off —a thing which could never have happened in the early days of internment. I think this acceptance may have been due partly to the fact that many of those who protested strongly about class distinction were now working outside the camp.

Another ripple on the placid surface of our lives was caused when a very low type announced that he was leaving the camp and going to Berlin to work for the Germans in some minor capacity. Unfortunately, as soon as this became known, the Germans placed him under their protection, otherwise he might have arrived in Berlin in little pieces. He received his just reward in prison when the War was ended.

Among friends, discussion often turned to the plight of those who were left behind in Guernsey, where we knew conditions were getting progressively worse. Thoughts of our loved ones on the mainland were constantly in our minds and the news we received from them was very reassuring, in most instances.

So the remainder of 1943 and the first six months of 1944 passed in a slow, turgid trickle of tranquillity—more or less—the great event of each evening being the arrival of the news bulletin. When D-Day burst upon us we woke up with a bang, and during the first phases of the invasion of Europe were concerned with speculation as to the time it would take the liberating forces either to force the enemy to plead for peace or to liberate us. Unfortunately for us, we were at the opposite side of the Reich from that which was nearer to the Western Allies.

When the Allied advance slowed down in the autumn we were disappointed, naturally, and when Christmas came —a far different affair from the Christmas of 1942—my prophecy of the hold-up of Red Cross parcels was entirely disproved, as the food continued to arrive regularly in the camp. The main question was: "How much longer?"

Von Runstedt's Ardennes offensive shocked us considerably and for a day or so, though no one said it openly, I am sure the thought at the back of everyone's mind was: "Shall we get out of here?" They were unhappy, disappointing days.

But we cheered up again when the offensive was crushed and the Allies renewed their advance. When this had really got into its swing, it was extremely difficult to keep track of the Allied armies as they moved towards the Reich and then into it. In particular we were amazed by the exploits of "Blood and Guts" Patton, as he dashed to the Rhine and over it. If he could keep this up he would soon be in our neighbourhood.

Inside the camp we were to become aware that the Germans were having attacks of the jitters. As the Allied advance developed, as happened in the areas where prison camps were located, the Gestapo began to be afraid of what reactions we might have to the good news. Though we were supposed not to be aware of the Allied operations beyond what they thought we should know, which was always coloured by their propaganda, they were not such idiots as not to give us credit for having a secret radio.

Our own German Camp Commandant, sensing increased Gestapo activity, and no doubt expecting thorough snap searches, probably feared drastic action being taken against his personnel as well as against the internees if a secret radio were found in his own back yard. He took matters into his own hands before the trouble materialised: acting with a high degree of humanity he took our Camp Senior, Ambrose Sherwill, into his confidence by informing him that if there were a secret radio being operated inside the camp a thorough search by the Gestapo would be certain to discover it. He confirmed that this would bring down indescribable reprisals on our heads and heavy punishment for the German camp staff. It was suggested, therefore, that if there was a radio it should be handed over to the British Camp Senior and he, in turn, could hand it over to the German office, where it would be put into custody under German protection, without any questions being asked.

Some time before this the Genius had discovered in the Y.M.C.A. stores a deaf-aid set that was capable of being converted into a wireless receiving set which provided us with a very good stand-by. We called it "Little Tich." There was a strong argument about whether we should surrender the "Forbidden Whisper" or not, and eventually it was decided that we should respect the Senior's wishes; I was sorry to have to part with it but I knew I would be the one for the "Ice Box" if it were found. I handed it over to my contact from camp office and it passed via the Camp Senior to the Germans.

We also decided to dismantle "Little Tich" for a time and he went back to Y.M.C.A. stores. The Gestapo did raid us but, naturally, found nothing. Within 48 hours of the "coast clear" the Germans handed back the Forbidden Whisper to the Camp Senior and it came back to me. I continued to receive authentic news, but without the same thrill as doing the Forbidden Thing.

As the situation began to become serious for the Germans, there seemed to be increased activity in the little town outside our camp. Reports began to come in from outside workers that the inhabitants of Laufen were very perturbed by rumours that the Nazis were preparing to make a last-ditch stand in the so-called Southern Redoubt centred on Hitler's eyrie at Berchtesgarten. As soon as we heard this we shared the people's anxiety, for we were within this area and had no desire to be involved in desperate fighting. To add to our troubles another piece of information from "reliable sources" came the way of camp office, who passed it on to the few who were in their confidence. It was alarming and more frightening even than the story of the Southern Redoubt. Whether it ever had a firm basis in fact is still not known, but at this time it fitted so well into the pattern of things as we knew them that we were prepared to accept it.

The story was that if the Southern Redoubt stand were actually put into effect, we in Laufen would be in the way of the German defenders. The S.S. were proposing, therefore, to herd us all into the cellars of the Schloss and then gas us. The thought of finishing up like this, after surviving the whole War and particularly at the time when the "Silver Lining" was at last breaking through, had a most disturbing effect on me personally, and I do not think I was alone with that feeling.

Fortunately, this information was closely followed by more news, which was that the Germans who had saved us from the Gestapo by taking our radio into their protection "no questions asked" were prepared to go to even greater lengths to help us now. The news also proved to us that the Germans were really divided among themselves and the more humane and responsible greatly opposed to the excesses of the S.S. This was particularly true of the Bavarians.

The news which consoled us a little was that the Commandant of the camp had let it be known that if the S.S. ever attempted to carry out their proposal to gas us, not only would he and his guards resist the S.S. by arms, but he would hand the few spare weapons he had to selected internees. As I said, this news cheered us a little, though we realised that even under those circumstances we should have little chance of survival unless help quickly came to us.

As the Americans dashed every day nearer and nearer to us, the camp seethed with rumours. We heard that they had liberated Dachau and had revealed to the world the ghastly things they had found there. This was followed by an unofficial report that Traunstein had been by-passed and, more encouraging still, that the women's prison at Liebenau was free and that a spearhead was approaching Laufen. Such was the speed of the advance that it was bewildering to us and to our guards alike.

Then came an order forbidding us to go near the windows, and this encouraged us to believe that help was, so to speak, coming up the road. When the Americans did, in fact, appear, no opposition was offered and before we knew quite what was happening we were being liberated.

Though this was what we had been hoping and praying for during these last three years, and had got ourselves worked up for in the last few days, when it happened we could scarcely believe it. There were a few who greeted the event with hilarity, but the majority of us were so thankful that we were dazed by our good fortune.

As a matter of fact we were extremely fortunate to be liberated when we were. The American C.O. had no idea that there was an internment camp in Laufen, and in his anxiety to move on was going to by-pass us. Now that he had found us he was taking no chances, and having the German staff, he decided to keep us confined to camp until he had orders from his superiors what to do with us. There was no use in blinking at the fact that the inhabitants of the Schloss were a very mixed bunch indeed, and that the Americans acted wisely when they refused to give us any freedom until all of us had been carefully screened. In the American section there were quite a few who failed to make the grade.

Apart from this sort of " security " angle, there was another aspect of our being allowed complete freedom. It would have been chaotic if all the liberated internees had descended on the little town of Laufen in one swoop. We had been shut up for three years and there were a number of young, virile and vigorous men among us. To be suddenly thrust into the outside world, with no one to say us nay, might easily have gone to our heads and got us into all sorts of difficulties. On the other hand, we did feel that we ought not to remain completely immured, and fortunately the Americans saw our point of view and arranged various outings for us at the first opportunity, one of which stands out vividly in my memory.

A number of us were invited to attend an all-American entertainment at Traunstein. Transport was provided in American service lorries, and early one afternoon we set off in high spirits. As we had not ridden in vehicles for some time, the sensation of travelling at speed was a little alarming and the alarm increased as the ride developed into a race between the lorries. Each lorry was jammed tight with humanity; some of us were sitting, some standing, and when we set off there was a sort of order among us, but as each corner was taken so we were thrown into ever-increasing disorder. The driver of the lorry in which I was travelling would have done himself credit at Le Mans or, alternatively, done himself in, for by taking every calculated risk (and many uncalculated ones) he kept his vehicle in the lead all the way. However, we arrived in one piece, if a little shaken.

We wandered at will round the town for a short time and were then entertained by our liberators. To round off the hospitality a feast of fried chicken, sweet corn and all the trimmings, which included snow white bread such as we had not seen for years, was set before us. At this point in

147

our lives, after eating out of tins for three years, this meal seemed unreal, dreamlike, though we were not averse to entering into the spirit of the dream and our tightening waistbands gradually proved the reality of our experience.

When the time came for the return journey, the colour drained from my cheeks as I heard our driver announce that the outward trip had taken too long and that he intended to clip a quarter off the homeward run. As I looked about me, I had good reason to believe that I was not the only one to suffer from similar reactions.

At the first corner we came to he almost clipped a quarter off his load. The lorry was an uncovered one except for the driver's cabin, and as we shrieked around the bend on two wheels, it seemed, overhanging boughs swept over us and only by the grace of providence were those standing not knocked off. In the pitch dark the journey became a nightmare, as the vehicle swayed from side to side and the tyres kept up an unremitting screech. The road was by no means an autobahn and I am convinced that it was only because our driver was blessed with the luck of the three blind nannygoats that we survived.

From the top of the hill down into Laufen he really gave us the " works " and to crown his performance, at the Schloss entrance he rammed on his brakes so late that only a cigarette paper could have passed between the radiator and the gates. The fierceness of our stop resulted in his human cargo shifting and crashing forward in a struggling, bruised mass. To add insult to injury the driver offered his apologies.

I for one felt, after this, that the security of the Schloss was far preferable to the dangers of American entertainment. Although we received other invitations, I found other diversions. I was able to hire a bicycle and on it I visited Salzburg and the surrounding countryside at my leisure. The saddle was not a Terry and I developed some quite painful blisters on my seat, but at least I came and went safely, at my own speed.

While we were waiting, plans were being made for us and if we were impatient to be gone this was only natural. At last the day came when we were told what was to happen to us.

Chapter XV

GOING HOME

IT HAS OFTEN SEEMED TO ME that the people whose names start with a letter near the top of the alphabet have a definite advantage over those whose initial is towards the end. Whether this is a fact borne out by research, I do not know, but it was certainly because my name begins with an S that my return to Guernsey was delayed.

Our joy can be imagined when our American liberators told us that an airlift would take us all home in one day. It would be laid on seven days from that day. To give me something to do, I made a graph of the days, hours and minutes that had to pass before this great event would take me back to England and to my loved ones, from whom I had been separated for five years—years of hope followed by disappointment and, again, from time to time, surges of new hope. Surely this time everything must go according to plan! Within seven days! Think of it, within seven days I would be home!

True to their word, on the seventh day a fleet of American Army transports arrived to take us all to Salzburg airfield. We piled in, complete with personal belongings and the Forbidden Whisper, in the highest of high spirits. The inhabitants of Laufen village turned out in strength to bid farewell to the men who had been their unwanted guests for almost three years, and amid a crescendo of cheers, the convoy moved off at gathering speed and raising great clouds of dust behind them. The men with initials low in the alphabet were, of course, loaded last and so caught the brunt of the miniature dust storm raised by preceding trucks. But no one minded. We were on our way HOME!

As Salzburg, at American Army speed, was less than an hour from Laufen, we soon arrived and were assembled on the airfield, where we began to work out the time we should be crossing over the white cliffs of Dover. But with every minute that passed we had to produce a new estimate. All the morning and until late in the afternoon we waited. Timeless minutes and unending hours went by and still no airlift. Reports from Control did little to help us, as nothing definite was known. By mid-afternoon we were right down in the dumps and some suggested that it would be quicker to walk, though the idea found little support.

Late in the afternoon the sight of planes approaching gave us new hope. Six large transport aircraft landed on the field and with typical American " go " the roll was called and loading began—starting, of course, with the letter A. By the time the first four letters of the alphabet had been called the planes were filled. Still, we were not unduly concerned for we felt that this was only the first flight of the day. But not on your sweet life! It was, in fact, the one and only flight for the day and after waiting hopefully until dusk we were told to return to the camp for the night. The air was filled with many impolite words and the disappointment, naturally, was great. I resolved that at the first opportunity I would change my name to Abrahams. Although we now had the freedom of the camp and were at liberty, the knowledge helped us very little that night and our thoughts dwelt mostly on the lucky blighters whose names began with A, B, C and D—and they were not very kind thoughts.

Next morning we were all ready and waiting for the transport long before they were due. But we wasted our time, for the air-lift for that day was cancelled. We were so fed up with this news that we " went out on the beer." The strength of the beer was about $\frac{1}{8}$ degree proof spirit and tasted, someone suggested, like Cleopatra's bathwater. But at least it passed the time and the truth of the old saying " what does not fatten, fills " was brought home to us.

Another night and morning passed. Then about midday transport arrived and with renewed cheer and some ironical remarks about being " back again tonight " we moved off amid more dust to the airfield. More planes arrived, the roll was called again and yet again there were not enough aircraft to reach the end of the alphabet. As, however, the number of those left over did not warrant the laying on of another plane, it was decided that each pilot should take off with two or three extra passengers. Everybody was happy then, until some bright lad suggested that it was doubtful whether, so loaded, the planes would clear the trees fringing the airfield. However, he proved to be unduly pessimistic and soon we were airborne on a course roughly N.N.W., heading for England, home and glory.

Without incident we came to and passed over that landmark so dear to Englishmen, the white cliffs of Dover, flew over that part of Kent that had become known as "Bomb Alley" and on to Hendon Airport. We touched down at the second attempt and at long last our feet were firmly on English soil.

Soon we had been issued with travel warrants to our various destinations, had five shillings pressed upon us to meet our immediate needs, received food from the Red Cross, which lived up to its great reputation right up to the last moment, and were told that we were free to continue on our way. Before we went, however, I do not think that there was one of us who did not take the opportunity to thank the Red Cross with deep and sincere gratitude for keeping us alive during our captivity.

I was pleasantly surprised to meet friends John and Ann Van Draege from Guernsey as I left the airport, and I shall always be grateful to them for insisting that I take money from them on loan, to be repaid at my convenience. Then, after telegraphing my family to warn them that I was on my way, I began the long train journey to the north.

To find words to suit the actual moment of reunion is beyond my literary ability. Even if it were not so, I should ask to be excused a description of this realisation of this five-year-old wish now, it seemed, almost miraculously come true. I must say, however, that my small daughter, meeting me for the first time within her memory, seemed to be slightly doubtful about accepting me. I think she was expecting to see someone closely resembling Errol Flynn, who at that time was her favourite film star, and if this is so, I must have been a bitter disappointment as far as looks went. I suppose mine was not an isolated experience. An unseen parent must become something of an ideal, and in anticipation the child naturally identifies the missing mother or father with the highest object of her admiration. However, when I had assured her that I was the spitting image of Errol Flynn's brother and that even her hero would look

151

more like me if he had spent three years in an internment camp, she began to accept me and from then on her confidence grew.

Naturally, too, my wife and I had a good deal to talk about. We conjured up incidents from the past, we thought of people from the island, we wondered—if we did not know —who had done well and who had done not so well during their sojourn in the Motherland and we remembered those who had died. Of course we had many stories to exchange of our own experiences.

But soon came the time when the future had to be considered and decisions had to be taken. And after the decisions came the period of waiting and of preparation.

I had no priority and so had to take my place on the waiting list. Once again I felt that my surname was not a help, but as I also knew that I was not the only one in this boat, I realised that I must be patient.

Eventually we were advised that my permit to travel would enable me to return to Guernsey via Southampton on such and such a date. As I was hoping that I would be able to start my business again with the least possible delay, I made hasty contacts and renewed as many business associations as I had time for.

I remember very little about the actual return journey home. I do recall, however, that I was on deck long before we reached the harbour. I had no intention of missing the sight of many once familiar landmarks which have served to guide the passage of ships approaching from the north from time immemorial and will no doubt remain until the end of time. I picked out many of these, including many man-made ones, but as we came nearer I realised that two outstanding ones were missing. They had been memorials to famous Guernseymen and had been demolished by the Germans so that no clandestine landing could be made with their help.

As I stood wondering why this had been done, since all the natural guides were still there, we came nearer to the harbour and I was almost home. It was a day in August, 1945, when at long last I stepped ashore in the island. But the sight that greeted me now was different from the last sight I had had of it. The harbour was still out of bounds to the inhabitants and the barricades were still in position.

But now it was German soldiers who were doing work previously undertaken by their captive forced labour. A detail was engaged on locating their own mines.

I wondered if by any good fortune the pompous little upstart who had organised the party in The Home from Home at Christmas, 1941, was among them. I could summon up no good will for him, although the war was now over. As soon as I could I tried to assess the damage done to Guernsey by the Germans and as I looked at the changes which had been forced among us, as a man in the street I thought we were lucky that the damage had not been greater than it was. True, we had many permanent memorials in the form of Nazi architecture which we could well have done without. These monstrous edifices lined our lovely coastline, spoiling the approaches to our picturesque bays, while inland they were so placed that they disfigured the landscape and lay waste valuable agricultural land, of which we were already short.

But as one who had reason to know, I felt sure that the greatest damage inflicted on us was in our morale. Many among us, who had lived in and loved Guernsey for the greater part of our lives, had been rudely shocked when made to realise that this small island of seven miles long and three miles wide could be considered a worthy prize for an invader. We had completely failed to consider the fact that because we were part of the English speaking world we had a value for the propagandists of the enemy. I had been as guilty of this as any other islander with similar views. I had grossly underestimated the value attached by others to this small part of the British Commonwealth which lay so close to the Motherland. In not realising these things, we had suffered much in our personal lives—the long break in our family life, the loss of our children's babyhood years. But there is no use in crying over spilt milk and it was all over now. Though we could not recall the lost time, we were at least fortunate in being whole in wind and limb, and, what was more, reunited.

The main cause of my anxiety to return to Guernsey as soon as possible was to find out what had happened to my affairs during my absence. Before I describe what I found, I should like to recall to mind my position at the time of my deportation to Germany. I had only myself to blame for not laying down a more conclusive policy to be followed by The Home from Home. I had asked my staff only to keep open as long as they could, or at least while there was still food to be obtained. Although the café had been kept open it had incurred substantial trading losses since no reasonable turnover could be achieved. These losses had eaten up much of the profit from the previous years, and although the stock of precious linseed oil, acorn coffee and other valued utility commodities was liquidated, the proceeds had not realised sufficient profits to meet running costs. However, its usefulness in keeping people employed must be taken into consideration.

In the period before my departure, and particularly in the early days of the Occupation, I had worked hard, not for the benefit of my health, but to clear up the shocking mess I had made of my businesses during my formative years. I had distributed my cash profits among several local firms with whom I had man-sized outstanding accounts. I am glad to say that by the time " Jerry " had taken me to see his home, I had liquidated all local debts, restored the status quo at the bank and, having put that on an even keel, been able to pay off a good round sum on the mortgage of the house. So all in all, I left Guernsey a well satisfied man, and not without the feeling that if " Jerry " had left me alone for the duration of his occupation I might have been able to accumulate a fair credit balance at the bank through my own efforts and initiative for the first time in my life.

I felt, too, that I should come home to make a fresh start free of all local liabilities when the War was over. Any additional profits I had made I had ploughed into stock in the hope of keeping the café going throughout the Occupation and though I proved wrong, I still hoped there would be a little left in the kitty which would permit me to kick off again. However, when I did return, the cash balance was non-existent.

Nevertheless, I was raring to go and the conditions were not unfavourable. Every effort was being made to get Guernsey back on her feet again as quickly as possible—" rehabilitation " was the favourite word then. The urge to spend was great, as people had been without for so long. The population was increasing daily as evacuees returned home. Nearly everyone you met had some tale of woe to tell about how the " Jerries " had done this or that to their house or furniture; or they had only received so much for their brand new car, which they had had to leave behind when they left for England; or old so-and-so had done them properly while they were away; or had you heard that old stick-in-the-mud's wife had come back with two-year-old twins; or that thingummy's wife was not coming back at all!

To the great majority, however, the events of the past five years were dead and buried. The thing that mattered was getting things straight again. The future was the stake, so why waste time chasing shadows of the past?

For me there was no thought of re-opening my café as the furnishings and fittings were not mine and the rightful owners were returning to the island and would want to get started themselves. Besides, I much preferred my pre-war business and had always looked upon the café as an Occupation stop-gap. However, I would have some very pleasant memories when I finally turned the key in the door.

So it was back to the old love but with the firm undertaking and determination that this time there was going to be no mess-up, and what better start could I have hoped for than a clean sheet and a period during which all goods were in short supply, so that whatever you bought you were sure of selling? Although this year it was too late and things were too unsettled for a visitor season, next year we would have a ready-made visitor traffic in the personal contacts made during the war years, when more than half our population was overseas. It really did seem to me a wonderful opportunity to get on my feet again, but I must not make a mess of it this time, I repeatedly told myself.

For some months it was heavy going and little real headway was made for several reasons. First, the firms in my particular trade which had had an executive in the island at the time of the Liberation, or had the capital to instruct some contact to buy for them for cash on the mainland, had a very great advantage over those like me who were starting from scratch and who had returned when the others were already established. Also, I had very little capital. For those on the spot it would be possible to secure goods offered by firms with pre-war contacts in the island. Besides, even if they were unable to secure goods for prompt delivery they would at least have the opportunity of making an early contact and be included in the next list of applications for allocations.

All this was impossible for people placed as I was and it took a few months before some firms would even consider starting to supply us. Our position was greatly eased, however, by the continued operation of the States of Guernsey Control of Essential Commodities Committee, which once more did a really excellent job in seeing that the more important stock was passed through the proper channels for fair allocations. In fact, I hesitate to think what would have happened to some businesses if this control had been relaxed. But it was in the non-essential classes of goods that the first-in cash bidder scored. As these types of goods were coming into an island starved for five years of all luxuries they found a ready, profitable market.

It soon became very evident to me that if I was going to rehabilitate myself successfully I must have some capital, and quick! So, at the first opportunity, I realised on the house, renewed acquaintance with the bank, where, in the spirit of the rehabilitation era, my wants and desires were accommodated to the limit of the powers vested in them. At least that was what they told me. but I have an idea that reference to my pre-war record was made and another crisis was not entirely overlooked as a possibility. But this help at least gave me an additional lift. Stocks were the primary factor at that particular time in my line of business; and as these were actually forthcoming, little by little things began to build up.

My family had now rejoined me and as we had disposed of the house, we lived in the flat above the main shop, intending to move on as soon as the position warranted it. This was a great economy and also gave the added advantage of having my wife's personal assistance in the business. This proved invaluable, for personal contact is always a main asset in the smaller type of business. It was necessary for me to work long hours but as I was at home it meant that we were together and it kept me away from the club.

Two developments in our return to normal happened in quick succession. As stock gradually returned to the local market, so did the sales of the States of Guernsey sales tax stamps increase to the benefit of the local Treasurer—and myself. The sales tax was really a form of purchase tax, and though many items were exempt there was a considerable call on the stamps by the shopkeepers. This procedure of using stamps greatly facilitated the collection of tax by the States, for the shopkeepers had to buy the stamps from the States, paying in advance. For this the States appointed a number of agents to sell the stamps on their behalf at a small commission, and I was one of the chosen few. Although the commission was more or less a token profit, that was not so important to me as the large cash turnover it gave me, of which I must admit, I took full advantage. At the same time, I was always able to scrape sufficient liquid assets to meet the account when it fell due.

The other important development from my point of view was the relaxation of travel restrictions which made it possible for businessmen to go freely backwards and forwards between the island and England. Then an air service operated and this helped me, too, since it was most important that my absences from the island should be as short as possible. By using the airways, I could leave Guernsey in time to keep a midday appointment in London and be back in Guernsey the same evening, if necessary. For a time I made the trip each week to open up some new contacts and to arrange for credit terms.

The reception I received from English business men varied widely and usually depended on the demand for the particular type of goods I wanted. But if I failed at the first approach, I didn't give up hope but would go back again two or three times; in fact, until I was received with " What, you again! " " How many more times are you going to bother us? " This I came to recognise as a sort of signal that this time I was going to be successful. In several instances, however, after my third or possibly fourth visit, it was quite clearly indicated to me that if I ever darkened their doors again I should find myself charged with committing a breach of the peace. Then I had no choice but to write that firm off my list.

That first year of peace in Guernsey was vital to all to whom rehabilitation meant everything. To the farmer it meant his return to rearing the pedigree cattle for which we are famed throughout the world, and which has always been the Guernsey farmer's first love. The grower was once again able to produce the tomato for export to England, and thus help to restore the island's economy. The hotelier was once again able to welcome guests who paid their accounts with real spending money. To the one-man business starting anew, it was the year in which to lay the foundation of his future.

I should be giving a false picture, however, if I gave the impression that life was just one long round of work. There was a social side to it, too, though it was kept strictly to a minimum.

The early days of our return were devoted, naturally, to meeting our friends in the island from whom we had been separated, either because they had stayed behind, or because they had been evacuated to different places in England. One of our reunion celebrations has left lasting impressions on both my wife and myself.

A social evening was arranged for us by a great friend of Occupation days, Len Collins, and his wife at one of the leading local hotels. My wife and I anticipated a quiet evening of reminiscing and within minutes of our meeting we were engrossed in our stories, sitting in the quiet lounge with our own particular favourite drinks by our sides. At this time celebrations were taking place to welcome visiting British warships and suddenly our peace was shattered by two naval ratings. Both were in the heavy-weight class and both were at least half-seas over.

They literally rolled into the lounge with great noise and at once started to abuse us. My wife's friend, trying to pass the incident off as a joke, received a smart backhander across the face which sent her spectacles flying across the room. Believing discretion to be the better part of valour, I stood up and tried to persuade the larger one and seemingly more reasonable of the two that we were not wanting trouble, and would they please go away. Unfortunately the other man had by now launched a frontal attack on my friend and having put him *hors de combat* in double quick time, he turned on me from behind. In but a few seconds I was defending myself from all sides but luckily in a clinch, the big man overbalanced and went down with me on top of him. After receiving several rabbit punches from No. 2 adversary, I managed to get up and beat a hasty retreat into the billiards room, followed closely by my two assailants. Several people were playing snooker and looked up from their game in amazement, but I think they must have thought I was indulging in a game of *ring-a-ring of roses,* for not one of them made any attempt to come to my aid and it was not until one of them had had his feet kicked out from under him that he understood the game and decided that there was no place in it for him.

While all this had been going on the doorman, who was only pint-size, and had been summarily swept aside by the ratings when he had attempted to bar their entry, had dashed out for the police and they, together with naval patrol men, now came to the rescue. Using commando methods they secured the offenders, and after the usual inquest apologies were tendered to the ladies present and we were given a personal assurance that justice would be done. I understand that our attackers did receive their just deserts, for it was then learned that it was their original intention to " bash the lights out of " an officer with whom they had found reason to disagree, who had been in the dining room of the hotel all the time. When order had been restored, we were approached by the management, who added their personal apologies to those of the naval authorities. Although up to that time we had felt extremely upset, we realised that the management was equally upset and concerned about the possible repercussions of a court action for damages. Our evening was ruined, however, for we could not settle down again though we were able to rebuild our confidence with the aid of a little dutch courage.

This incident occurred in the Royal Hotel where, before the War, it had been almost necessary to have executive status before being allowed to pass the portals. It made me wonder if there was not something to be said in favour of the protection provided by an internment after all.

In my younger days I had tried practically every form of sport with varying degrees of success. Now I had reached an age when strenuous exercise was too much like hard work, but still I had to have exercise, so I decided to try my hand at the Royal and Ancient game. The changes which our recent experiences had wrought in our social organisation had brought membership of the local Golf Club within reach of people in my station of life. Before World War I, I have been told, you practically had to produce your birth certificate and pass a blood-test before being admitted to membership, but now if you were a shareholder in the Co-op you were welcome.

Having heard and read quite a deal about this famous game while in Germany, and having watched internees hitting an imaginary ball with an invisible club, the urge to play took a strong hold on me as soon as I considered it. So, after receiving advice from all quarters, and being assured that I had only to keep my head down to get into single figures in next to no time, I began to learn this intriguing game. Now, after two years' play, the only success I can claim is the record score for one hole on the local course.

On our course, at L'Ancresse, there is a bogey four hole, No. 12, flanked by formidable bunkers. The approach to the green is very narrow. Out one day, I reached the opening to the green in three shots and was ultra cautious with my approach shot. Possibly because I was too cautious, I steered the ball into the deep bunker. It took me 16 shots to get out of the bunker and into the opposite bunker via a gorse bush, eventually to reach the green, when at last the ball disappeared into the hole. I had registered a neat 21 shots which, as I have said, is a record for that hole.

After standing drinks all round to record the removal of an unprecedented amount of sand from the bunker, I had second thoughts about the game in general and my own chances of ever being able to play it, in particular. So I decided to give it another six months or 50 golf balls' trial (my normal wastage being four balls per round). I then had the temerity to enter a competition specially staged for the awkward squad. My opponent in the first round failed to put in an appearance so I sailed into the second round. By the time we had reached the 16th hole some three hours after driving off at the first, I had concluded that I was the equal of my opponent, except in the range of language he could employ to describe certain of his shots. As, all square, we teed up for the 17th hole, our one spectator remarked what a good game it was; to which my opponent suitably replied. We halved that hole and the outcome rested on the 18th.

When he had spent some time telling his ball exactly what he expected of it, and describing what would happen to it if it did not behave as he wanted it to, my opponent drove off. The ball followed his instructions to the letter and landed well inside the green. I then carried out all the preliminaries and my drive followed a true course, but then seemed to disappear. For the second time in my life the fact that cows have a certain nuisance value became obvious to me. My opponent regarded my plight sympathetically but while commiserating with me, laughed like a drain all the time. Rule or no rule, I appealed to his gentlemanly instincts to permit me to remove the ball on to firmer ground, but he positively refused to let me touch it unless I awarded him the game. He advised me to scrape round it but if I as much as shook the ball, he would claim the game.

Members watching from the club house wondered at the delay, as did the pair following immediately behind us. The latter grew impatient and their shouts of " fore " forced me into a snap decision. If I scraped as advised, I should have to bring a bull-dozer up, so large was the offending area. (I could only imagine what a magnificent beast had been there). Further warning " fores " made up my mind for me. Urging my opponent and the solitary supporter to stand well clear I tied a handkerchief over my mouth and nose and surveyed as closely as possible the angle at which the entry had been made. Only by so doing could I judge where the ball was at all.

Closing my eyes and firmly using a wedge, I struck more in hope than anger; the ball rose majestically and, hey presto! landed within two feet of the pin. My opponent, being lost for words, missed his putt, so we halved the match. At the convivial 19th hole an inquest resulted in a divided opinion on the correct course to be taken in the event of a ball being submerged as mine had been.

Our first Christmas was a memorable one. The luxuries which we were able to purchase and which had certainly not been seen in Guernsey during the last five Christmasses, seemed to the children too good to be believed. Although many families were saddened by the one or more vacant chairs and their sorrow was shared by all those who were aware of their losses, the true spirit of Christmas returned to Guernsey. The months which follow the New Year always seem to drag, but passed pleasantly as we waited for the season to begin. This coming season was to see the realisation of our hopes and of the work done. It was to be the first link in the chain of our future progress. It was to restore not only the island to its rightful place in the sun but ourselves to normal life once more.

CHAPTER XVI

VICTORY MARCH

I SUPPOSE THERE ARE EVENTS IN everyone's life the recounting of which gives a renewed thrill. One such event in my lifetime was the Victory March through London to celebrate final victory. It took place in May, 1946, and the contingent from the Channel Islands included representatives from Jersey, Guernsey and Sark. As Alderney had been totally evacuated at the time of the partial evacuation from Guernsey, there was no resident that could represent the Northern Island.

I felt highly honoured when an official-looking envelope was delivered by hand, and on opening it I found an invitation to be a Guernsey representative for this historic event. The days that followed passed in pleasant and excited anticipation.

When the great day at last arrived, the party assembled at the airport, to be flown to Jersey to join the party from that island. This was necessary because the York aircraft of the King's Flight which had been provided needed a longer take-off run than Guernsey airport could allow. There was no repetition of the Salzburg delays this time, and in a few minutes they were on their way. I was already in London and met them there.

Unhappily, the day chosen for the event was badly let down by the weather, and the huge gathering in Hyde Park had its ardour somewhat dampened as it waited to move off. But the thought that this was indeed our day soon took charge of the spirits and we decided to ignore the rain.

After what seemed like an eternity, the distant strains of a military band warned us that the head of the procession was on the move and that the time was approaching for us to join the procession. Presently we were marshalled by a Guards officer, who was obviously not used to handling such undisciplined types, and his efforts to apply squad drill tactics were wasted. But eventually he got us into some sort of shape and we fell into our allotted places.

From the moment we were in formation I realised that something was lacking in our contingent. Every other unit possessed some mark of recognition, such as a flag or banner, or uniform. But we had nothing to signify whether we came from the Channel Islands or the Solomons, except, perhaps, the colour of our skins and the fact that we wore thick shoes. There had no doubt been some unfortunate misunderstandings or someone had forgotten, but for many of us it took away much of the glamour from the cause we represented.

It was a truly inspiring sight to see the representatives from every far-flung outpost of our great Commonwealth of Nations gathered together in the great reunion. These were the men and women who had contributed their mite to the final victory and who represented all the millions of their fellows who had similarly served mankind. Now their services were to be recognised by their King, the Royal Family and the population of the capital of the Motherland.

I could not help thinking about our lack of identification, particularly as I was sure that many thousands of people lining the route were friends of the islands and had watched our trials and tribulations of the last five years with great sympathy. Though probably they themselves had suffered in other ways, I was sure they would have been pleased to give the representatives of " our dear Channel Islands " as the great architect of victory, Winston Churchill, had called us, a big reception, for we had been the only truly British soil to be trodden by the jackboot.

Not by any stretch of the imagination could even our proudest member claim that we were a smart turn-out or that our marching set the parade a high standard, but at least we tried. We might have achieved better results had the same band played non-stop, but after we had succeeded in getting into step with a military band then a marine contingent took over and disorganised our tempo and our stride. But it was when there was no music at all that the real trouble came.

Looking down our line from my position on the left wing, it seemed as if our inside forwards had dropped back to help the defence. Then when the music started up again, we gradually straightened up until we look like an eight-prong attack. As we wheeled, the formation looked like a dog's hind leg, but with a little hop, skip and a jump, the extreme wheelers caught up with the insiders and then with a united double shuffle, we fell into time with the band. The party in front was having similar trouble and all along the line the non-professional marchers were having their difficulties. I am sure that the number of double shuffles and hop-skip-and-a-jump manoeuvres would have blurred any aerial photograph of the parade. But who among us cared? We were just Jack, Jill, Jenny or Mary, and our occupations ranged from the professional men-at-arms, to the supporting services of the forces and the fire-fighters and bomb-disposers through the whole organisation of services essential to a nation at war, the men in the factories, the mines and on the farms. In fact, we were the representatives of the people who, through the long, dark years of war, had derived inspiration from the leader who could promise nothing but " Blood, sweat, toil and tears." With that to urge them on, they had won through to victory. Not only were we of widely varied vocations, but we were from all over the world. It was an education in itself to see how far was flung the loyalty to our Crown and flag. We were all members of this great Commonwealth of Nations and this parade was OUR parade.

The absence of our party's emblem was not commented on by the crowd until we halted at the end of Oxford Street before wheeling right into Charing Cross Road. Although we were received well, as was every other unit, I still thought we ought to have something to identify us. But it was from the windows of Frascati's Restaurant, as it was then, that our identity was first questioned by some wise guy who shouted: " Say, where do you mugs come from? " I had been expecting just such a question ever since we had passed out of Hyde Park and I had thought of a reply. It came out now, as I had buttoned it up too long: "Wormwood Scrubs" I shouted back.

My reply was greeted with loud cheers, but at least it helped to ease the pain of a verruca which I had on my heel and which up to that moment had been giving me trouble. After this pause we moved off to the loudest cheer we had so far received.

By the time we reached Cambridge Circus we were all at sixes and sevens, which was caused chiefly by a very enthusiastic lady with a bevy of beauties—I believe it was Cicely Courtneidge and her company who were cheering from the balcony of a theatre in Charing Cross Road. The sight of so much concentrated beauty distracted our attention from our marching and as a result the rear rank attempted to overtake the front rank and my verruca made contact with someone's boot, which caused me to do a very quick double shuffle.

The climax, of course, was marching past the royal saluting base. From the moment we left Trafalgar Square and entered the Mall through Admiralty Arch, the whole character of the march seemed to change and the cheering seemed louder and different. Now everyone seemed most anxious to obey the order "eyes front"—"for goodness' sake get in step and stop mucking about and swing your arms as though they belong to you! " Just before the great moment of marching past His Majesty, every one of us seemed to be resolved not to let the side down and, taking our bearings from the left marker, we did a smart eyes-left and received the royal acknowledgment.

With the great moment over, we must have relaxed considerably. The strain of the long march had taken its toll of the older members of our party and when we came to the end of the trail we looked like Farmer Brown's cows coming in for the night.

Many forms of entertainment had been organised for us in the evening, but I preferred to roam casually among the familiar land marks. I went up to St. Paul's Cathedral and stood marvelling for some time at the seemingly divine protection which had been accorded that great symbol of our Christian faith, for it stood in a sea of devastation and ruin.

On our return journey our pilot made a complete circuit of St. Helier. Having given us the opportunity of seeing and being seen, he then landed us in our great plane, and from the sister island we made our way home.

Every member of the party felt that on that day they had received a signal honour in being chosen to represent their island, but it was not the personal honour which we took delight in; rather was it the honour done to our island by the recognition of all that it had suffered and stood for in this period of its history which we sincerely hope will never be repeated.

Chapter XVII

AND NOW . . .

A LITTLE MORE THAN TEN YEARS have passed since the last event I have described in the preceding chapters. Today happens to be New Year's Day and as the weather has been spring-like in its sunshine and warmth, I decided to walk in the town. As I came to a spot from which there is a magnificent view, I stopped to take in the full beauty of the scene, and realised how different everything had looked when I had stopped here, as I had done often, during the German Occupation. Then, there had been a sense of loss of freedom; but today there was no limit to anything.

The Casquets Rock, with its lighthouse, and the island of Alderney stood out on the horizon, clear-cut, free and with an air of self-assurance. To the north-east, and stretching to the south as far as the eye could reach, the coastline of France was clearly visible and it, too, seemed to breathe with freedom. Very much closer were the lovely little islands of Herm and Jethou, bathed in sunshine, full of life and adorned in many colours. Behind them, as though protecting them from the east winds, Sark was lying serene and tranquil in the blue sea.

Directly below me was the harbour of which we are so proud. As I watched, the mailboat was nosing her way out to begin her daily journey to the Motherland, and it reminded me of that July day, nearly 17 years ago, when I watched the ship take my wife and little daughter from me.

Turning to the north I was surprised to see that the lowlands were still shrouded in mist. But gradually the sun was chasing the mist away and soon the whole island began to sparkle like a great diamond, as the rays of the sun struck glasshouses and were reflected.

I stood for a while, watching and thinking, and then it was time for me to move on. As I made my way down into the town I was amazed by the number of television aerials. Was I in the wrong trade? I wondered.

As I came nearer to the centre of the town, I found many people to greet. I passed through that part which, in times past, was known as the "tough" area, and where the Germans had housed their forced labourers, and I had recalled that during the Occupation it had reminded one of the Kasbah. But what an improvement now! I could not resist standing for a moment to take in the beauty of a newly built granite wall. It is a superb wall and I thought what a pity it was that all our walls cannot be built of our own Guernsey granite.

As I glanced at the clock on the Town Church I realised that I had dallied too long on the way and that I am already too late for the time-honoured custom of the Bailiff's reception. On the first morning of the New Year large numbers of Guernsey's men of substance and of ordinary men-in-the-street, too, call to pay their respects to our island's civic chief. When they have shaken hands with him they pass into his chambers to take a glass of wine.

In the crowded space greetings are exchanged with all and sundry by all and sundry. Then at mid-day the Lieutenant-Governor, the Sovereign's representative in the island, proposes the Loyal Toast.

Leave is then taken of our host and we pass on to the Bureau des Connétables, where the greeting is extended by the town's two leading men, who are attended by the Douzaine, the town's "wise men." Once again there is wine and toasting and, one by one, we take our leave and go home.

I do not know of any other place in the world where this custom still exists. But I, personally, see in these New Year morning calls one of the great remaining symbols of Guernsey life. They began very many years ago and have continued without a break except for the years that the hosts of Adolf the house-painter were here. They symbolise the true Guernsey, the friendly isle, the island that loves to be loved.

What better place is there on earth to live, than Guernsey?

Frank Stroobant, May 1957.

167

OTHER BOOKS PUBLISHED BY BURBRIDGE

SIBYL, DAME OF SARK

"A lady of unusual personality" is how a Government official once described Dame Sibyl Hathaway of Sark. The world knew her as the tough yet benevolent feudal head of a small, beautiful Channel Island where cars, aeroplanes and divorce are still forbidden and life moves at a different pace. But this is by no means the complete story. There were frequent confrontations with officialdom and the church, private griefs and disappointments over her own large family and strong criticisms of some of her actions from the Sark people themselves.

Despite everything, she remained firmly in control — even during the German occupation of her island in the Second World War, an exciting story in itself. It was largely due to her efforts and the publicity that always surrounded La Dame that fame and prosperity came to Sark.

Barbara Stoney's thorough research has produced a fascinating and highly readable picture of a vital, complex woman from her stormy childhood, early runaway marriage and widowhood, to her accession in 1927, remarriage two years later and her death in 1974 at the age of ninety when all who knew her felt the loss of a formidable woman whose life had been every bit as colourful as that of her privateering ancestors.

Barbara Stoney is the author of the widely acclaimed biography of Enid Blyton. Sibyl, Dame of Sark is as totally absorbing and as shrewdly judged.

THE SILENT WAR

Frank Falla was a newspaperman in Guernsey when German forces occupied the Channel Islands in 1940. This is his story. He describes how for three years he and his colleagues fought Nazi censorship. He relives his days as a contributor to the underground news sheet and reveals the identity of the man who betrayed them and had them sent to German prisons. Finally, he tells of the disillusionment many Channel Islanders faced on liberation, as well as their joy at the freedom they had fought for so consistently.

But The Silent War is, above all, very readable, and is illustrated with many previously unpublished photographs.